Tea Tree Gully Library Writers' Group

Glimpses 3

Anthology 2018

Glimpses 3: Anthology 2018 Tea Tree Gully Library Writers' Group
ISBN 978-0-9945990-4-9

First Published in Australia 2018 by Sunshine Press

Cover Design: James Hickey
Book Design: Connie M. Berg
Editors: Rick Coy, Jan Stringer

Foreword

One of the first tasks I had when I was elected Mayor in 2014 was to write in the Library Writers' Group's Anthology of that Year. I am pleased to be asked, once again, to write the "Foreword" for this their latest publication, *Glimpses 3: Anthology 2018.*

This is an historic document because it heralds a new era. From this year onwards, the Tea Tree Gully Library Writers' Group will publish their material digitally on their new website. There will be a link to this on the Council's website.

The City of Tea Tree Gully is proud of the work the Library Writers' Group does and the valuable contribution they make to the cultural life and diversity of our community. In this the final anthology in this format, you will find all sorts of interesting articles, poems and short stories. Please enjoy your reading.

Kevin Knight
Mayor
City of Tea Tree Gully

Table of Contents

Ida Lee

Ida has been a long-time member of the SA Writers Centre as well as our group. Over the years she has been a campaigner for various causes and had her fingers in lots of pies. Her motto has always been, “Let what you know inspire you.”

Storm Chaser

by Ida Lee

There was a storm coming. A storm that would end up being the worst ever recorded in South Australia. He had done all the checking, all the model signs, indicators, cloud readings, thermal imaging and anything else he could think of. The signs were all there. He had studied everything for the last five days and was determined to record it if possible.

Jason Bourne is a Storm Chaser. He had never wanted to be anything else. Ever since he and his father had gone to the movies to see “Twister” when he was five years old. Now it looked as though he was about to have one of his own.

When he was younger and unable to drive a car, friends, or his parents were always able to get him to the places he wanted to be ... right in the middle of it all. Now, at age twenty, he had his own car and was able to take off to record any storms that approached.

It was the beginning of October 2016. Two days before the approaching storm. Jason phoned me and told me that this one was in the category of a ‘High Precipitation Super Cell’. These, he told me, were his favourites. He knew he had to be ahead of the storm and as close as he could possibly get. He also would have to find a reasonable place to park. He set to, mapping out his plans. He was hoping against all odds that he would get some very graphic pictures. His decisions were not to be taken lightly. He knew the dangers.

The storm was heading south, Crystal Brook, Red Hill, Spalding, Clare and Blythe were all waiting to hear if they were going to be in its path. Quite a lot of families took ultra measures and evacuated, leaving their homes behind and hoping against all hope that they would still be standing upon their return.

Two days before the storm hit, Jason knew, without a doubt, that it was going to come very close to Blyth. There had been a possibility that it might just miss the town, but he doubted it and wasn't going to miss this chance.

He prepared his car. Hooked up a movie camera. He made sure his mobile phone was near at hand and as an afterthought, put his iPad on the passenger seat within easy reach. He was determined to be able to record all aspects of the storm.

With nerves jumping he waited out the next two days, checking several times each day his monitors and charts. He read the weather patterns carefully. Nothing changed.

He had been up since day-break, preparing his car, making sure one last time that he had all the necessary equipment. Too nervous to eat breakfast, he left home early. His parents nervously saw him off, firing words of wisdom and anything else they could think of to help ease their own fear. They knew he was heading into danger but nothing they could say or do would have been able to stop him. Jason was on the mission of a lifetime.

He drove to Balaklava, turning north. A sudden cloud burst caused wind and rain to belt hard against the windscreen of the car, making it almost impossible for him to be able to see the road. He drove very carefully into Saddleworth. This, he thought, would be a quicker road to Blyth. Once there, he could stop, take time to prepare and assess his thoughts and feelings. On arrival at the outskirts of Blyth, he would find an area as close to the town as possible, safely park and film the on-coming storm. This was his plan and he methodically proceeded to set it into place.

He laid his precious movie camera on the seat beside him, turned on his phone and iPad, so that anything he said would be recorded. Then he carefully drove on.

As he neared the entrance to the Main Street of Blyth his heart began to thump wildly. What he saw both terrified and excited him. He pulled the car to the side of the road, making sure he could turn around for a quick get-away. The rain was easing. He could see ahead clearly.

"Holy Cow," he shouted. "Dad, you should see this. It's bloody awesome! Unbelievable! Dad! Mum! Fucking hell!" His excited voice was getting higher and higher. "I don't believe this! I've got to get pictures of this," he yelled as he frantically grabbed his movie camera.

His recordings were extremely frightening. A huge twister, looking terrifyingly like a massive grey water-spout was bearing down on the little town. The sky had turned a murky grey-black, then back to a messy dark grey. The rain stopped, as suddenly as it had begun. Was it because all the rain had been sucked into this monstrous apparition that was coming towards him at a terrifying speed? High above the houses the huge water-locked spout appeared to hover, a vortex of huge dimension covering half the visible sky.

From where Jason stood, alongside his car, filming and recording, the tornado looked massive. A huge swirling mass at the top, tapering down to a narrow spiral at the bottom approximately twelve metres across. And that was only what he could see over the roof tops. It appeared to take up most of the horizon and a deafening noise preceded the storm. He was both terrified and excited as he shouted into his phone and iPad. Somehow he managed to hold his camera as well.

The little town was directly in the tornado's terrifying path.

He was unable to say anything for the next few minutes. He was frantically filming, using his camera to capture the devastation that was happening ahead of him. Sheets of iron flew into the air then crashed to the ground, sliding all over the road, then again soaring into the sky, lifting as easily as sheets of paper only to suddenly disappear from sight. A large water tank rolled down the road, stopping against an iron garage that had been blown into the street. Trees were almost lying on the ground, branches tearing off, lifting like feathers then disappearing into the void.

Jason kept filming for what seemed like an eternity to him. Eyes wide, some might say babbling and swearing but filming non-stop.

"God in Heaven," he suddenly screamed. "There goes the whole bloody church roof. Dad! Mum! I have to get out of here now!" His shouts could be heard above the roaring of the storm.

He Jumped into the car, dropped his camera on the seat beside him, turned, and fled towards Clare; his only safe avenue at that stage. He drove for about fifteen kilometres before stopping to tell his parents that he was completely out of harm's way.

"I'll wait here a while, then go back to see if there is anything I can do to help."

In due course he did go back. He took more pictures of the devastation spread out in all directions. Trees had been ripped from the ground and tossed aside like match sticks. A group of local men approached him, asking for help to shift the iron garage back across the road. He did this willingly, feeling glad to help in some small way.

Later, whilst walking down the debris-strewn street, he helped other people to gather up the sheets of iron and splintered wood. The tank was nowhere to be seen. He was amazed that all this seemed to have taken place in such a short time. It felt like hours to him and incredible as it seemed, no-one had been seriously injured during all this horror.

What were his thoughts as he drove home? Elation? Horror? He was concerned about the poor folk who lived in Blyth.

Jason gave a very graphic description about his filming of the tornado and its path of destruction in an interview for the television news that night. He apologised for swearing so much during the making of the film but added it was really awesome. He admitted he was scared stiff most of the time but thankful for the opportunity to do what he loves most.

This is based on a true story. Jason is my grandson. I am very proud of him. And I would like to thank him for allowing me to write this story and to use his real identity. We wonder what his next expedition will be. Maybe storm chasing in America, or perhaps an exciting adventure to a volcano. Who knows? It's a big exciting world out there. We hope he will always come home safely.

Buttercup's Holiday
by Ida Lee

Can I like my buttercup van?
I might, I might, I know I can.

She pops and groans going up a hill,
Does this mean she needs a pill?

She huffs and puffs to reach the top,
Will she stop? Oh! Will she stop?

Reaching the top with a beaming smile,
Over she goes, driving down for a mile.

Around the bends she twists and turns,
The driver watches, the driver learns.

Through the towns and down to the sea,
My little Buttercup pleases me.

We stop for a night in a caravan park,
The sun goes down, it's getting dark.

On go the blinkers to block out the light,
Good night! Good night! Good night!

With the dawn comes excitement and toil,
First give me petrol, then give me oil.

We're off! We're off! The excitement builds,
Past houses, shops and very large fields.

Rivers, birds, white clouds on high,
Did we see some cows nearby?

Glimpses 3

A driver waves as we pass him by,
"Gosh!" moans the driver, "I'm feeling dry."

"A cup of tea, Buttercup, shall we stop? "
We shall, we shall, it's getting hot.

Some shade we find, right under a tree,
Up goes the top, a cuppa for you, a sleep for me.
Zzz! Zzz!

Well, that was nice I have to say,
The top comes down and we're away.

The rain gets heavy, the sky gets dark,
We have to find a place to park.

I'm looking, looking, everywhere,
Looking here and looking there.

My lights are on, I'm beginning to slow,
Oh where will I go, where CAN I go?

Before we've gone another mile,
My driver's face lights up with a smile.

Rounding a corner, a familiar red phone,
Buttercup honks, we're right near home.

We drive up the driveway, right into the shed,
I don't know about you mate, but for me it's my bed.
Good night! Good night!

Jessica Bate

Jessica is one of only two Life Members of our group. She was a founding member 25 years ago. She was an English teacher until she kicked the habit. Born in England, Jessica has lived in Australia for 30 years. She has had stories, poems and articles either published or broadcast in England, Australia and New Zealand. She has won a sprinkling of small prizes including in 1980 the H.E. Bates award for a story so depressing it was twenty years before she got any magazine to publish it!

Tomorrow
by Jessica Bate

Tomorrow
a mosquito, landing on my cheek,
will kiss me, gently,
and go on its gold-winged way.

Tomorrow
the news bulletins will be full
of man's humanity to man
and no-one will slaughter anyone.

Tomorrow
the ozone layer will laugh
in our frightened faces
and stitch itself together again.

Glimpses 3

Tomorrow
the fowlers will feed their sandwiches
to the wild ducks, sitting together
under a sky bright with flying pigs.

Tomorrow
you will say there was no truth
in your world-ending letter.

Tomorrow
you will promise to love me, always,
and I will believe you.

The Back Story
by Jessica Bate

In the Twenty-second Century nuclear weapons became, like phones and computers, a lot smaller. It was said that the missing 'White Bomb', if detonated, could destroy….well, not perhaps the entire world, but certainly the Western Hemisphere! It could apparently have been carried in a smallish suitcase, and very few people even knew what it looked like!

The loss of the White Bomb occurred when Clifford Strathborn was still working for the Nuclear Fuel Power Board. He himself retired soon afterwards, and secreted himself in Butterfield, a quiet, leafy area in southern England.

He became as far as possible, a non-person. A quiet, intelligent man, he showed no emotion. But there was one thing that was not known to anybody. There was a 'back story!' Benjamin, a local man in late middle age, managed to befriend Clifford, claiming old acquaintance at school. Benjamin one day said to Clifford: 'And what is your view of life?'

Clifford replied, coldly: 'I have no view of life. I think that existence is pointless.'

Benjamin, who should have known better, returned: 'If life, your life, is pointless, why don't you end it?'

'End my own life? That would be such a trivial act. My life is of no importance. If I wanted to 'make a gesture', so to speak, it would need to mean something! To have some significance!'

As I have said, there was a 'back story.' Clifford was in fact, a misanthrope. He had inside himself a deep hatred of life itself, born perhaps of his long association with weapons of mass destruction. As you may well have surmised by now, Clifford had himself stolen the White Bomb. It was hidden in a secret vault in his own house. Sometimes he went and looked at it, with half love, half hatred. 'One day' he said to himself, 'there will come the RIGHT day.' Yes, one day he would do it. When all the signs were there, when the world was clearly planning, by its own folly, to set in motion the slide into universal horror. Then HE, Clifford, would decide that it was time to end it all.

A small war broke out in Afghanistan over a trivial insult. He became alert! Was this the time? No! An interfering do-gooder established peace talks. Then, from Antarctica, came rumours that the Swiss, that country of most unlikely war mongers, claimed to have planted under an iceberg a weapon that would destroy the world! This was proved to be merely a piece of fake news! Then came a time when as once before two opposing arsenals faced each other at sea. Now! He thought. Now! He glanced at himself in the mirror, and smiled slightly. Good, surely, to have it over! He looked almost tenderly at the White Bomb, and pressed the button. Nothing happened! He pressed again, frowning. Nothing, no movement at all! A memory stirred in him. How could he have forgotten? The reason the White Bomb was so named was because it had a 'Best before' date!' Because of memories of Hiroshima and its long aftermath, the White Bomb had a 'use by date' after which it would become a chunk of useless metal!

Feelings churned in his head! What now? What was his purpose? He didn't know. Only one thing emerged. What he wanted to do was - to talk to Benjamin about it! Benjamin, he had said to him one day: 'Clifford, I sense that there is inside you a deep unhappiness. Here is my phone number. If you ever want to talk about it, ring me!' Yes! He could do that. Talk! Not perhaps about the bomb, but about his own feelings, the hatred inside him! He dialled the number. Benjamin came, and reaching out, gripping him strongly. Clifford talked and talked and talked.

Benjamin asked: 'But did you never realise what this hatred inside you was?'

'No! I just – always felt that life itself was - distasteful, pointless.'

It was strange, the sort of friendship he felt for Benjamin. He did not go in for friends! His one foray into the field of relationships with women was unpleasant to remember! No, no women! He recalled from long years before, the friend of his pre-teen years... Michael, he had been called! The only person in his life, towards whom he had felt a strong attachment. Almost...love. Though of course blokes don't talk of love for another bloke! He recalled when Michael's father got a new job and the family were to move, just once, the two boys had embraced each other! He had felt, what? Desire? surely not! He couldn't have. He couldn't.....then it was as though a wall inside himself began to tumble. He felt a stirring in his body and his face burned! Of course, if it was so, if he was – what was that word he recalled that they had used in the last century - gay? Was he – gay? Not that in this present age there was any kind of stigma attached. He recalled from his reading that way back, those strange old people a century ago had tried to legislate against, er, what was it? Single sex marriage? He felt no horror at himself, only strangeness, as though he was walking in territory unknown to him. And now Benjamin was here, smiling at him. He – he could talk to Benjamin, about anything, surely. When he had finished talking about the hatred, Clifford said. 'And there is one more thing I would like to tell you, Benjamin, my friend...'

'I thought there might be,' said Benjamin. He reached out and hugged him, just as all those years ago he and Michael had hugged, but he had not understood! He knew now what the back story really was. It was not hatred, but love.

Trevor Schaefer

Trevor has been a member of the group for seven years and in that time has established himself as a keen writer. He has published several church histories and a novel. As a librarian, he works constantly with words and books. He writes because he always has and he loves the creativity of it.

The Stranger

by Trevor Schaefer

The stranger came at the end of the wet season, a summer's day, through driving rain, the last downpour of the season, walking from the coast and carrying an umbrella over his head. He was dressed from head to heels in fine silk, a shirt and matching pants, decorated with an intricate pattern of dragons and pearls. On his head was a large hat from which dangled a single long feather. Only his feet were bare. The rain tumbled off the edges of the umbrella in little waterfalls and the shower was so heavy they could not distinguish him clearly from the umbrella. Through the streaming water, he looked like some sort of monster with an oversized head.

This strange apparition put them on alert and one man grabbed his spear and pointed it at the intruder.

"Stop there!"

They were completely taken aback when he called to them in their own language:

"Don't worry, it's only me."

The man with the spear was not satisfied. He held the spear at the intruder and replied,

"You may sound like one of us, but you don't look like one of us."

The stranger smiled. He stopped and threw down his umbrella. There were gasps from a few young children. Then, standing in the pouring rain, he stripped off down to his skin and put his hands out, palms open, to show he had no weapons.

They looked at him amazed. The man slowly lowered his spear and walked carefully towards him. He walked right around the stranger before he reached out to touch his skin. Then his face broke into a broad grin and he said, "He's one of us." Then the others ran over and crowded around him, each one touching his skin.

A child picked up the umbrella, and holding it over his head, laughed at the sudden shelter from the rain. The other children crowded under the umbrella and shrieks of laughter ensued as one and then another was pushed back out into the shower.

Meanwhile, a woman picked up the discarded shirt and gasped at the smooth, silky feel of the fabric. Someone else grabbed up the pants and held the silk cloth to her skin, saying, "Oooh!" Several pairs of hands snatched at the clothes.

"Don't fight," said the stranger, "I have plenty more of those in trunks down by the beach, and much else besides."

They looked at him in puzzlement, as they had no idea what a trunk was. He tried to explain:

"It's like a ..." But they had no word for a box or a lid. He tried again.

"It's like a...canoe, for things instead of people, and there's another canoe on top to keep the water out. We use them to store things on the big sailing ship, or, big canoe."

But they still looked puzzled.

Then the rain stopped suddenly and the sun came out from the clouds, blazing on the group and raising mist from the sodden ground.

"Come down and have a look," he cried and turned around to walk back the way he had come.

They all followed him down to the beach to view these new treasures.

Metamorphosis

by Trevor Schaefer

Slowly, he woke as if from a deep, deep sleep. As he regained consciousness he became aware that he ached all over, in every limb of his body. He seemed to be squeezed into a space too small for him, like a coffin. When he opened his eyes, it was pitch dark. A feeling of panic overwhelmed him and he tried desperately to free himself. As he wriggled and stretched his limbs, the confines began to give way, to stretch and to tear. Blinding light struck his eyes.

He clambered out of the now broken cocoon into the brilliant light. He blinked his eyes; no he didn't – he couldn't. These eyes were not just in front of his head, they weren't just in the back of his head, they were all over his head. He could see everything that moved around him, the leaves of a tree, the water rippling below, the ants crawling on the shore, the mosquitoes buzzing around, all at the same time.

His legs were wobbly, unused to moving, and he clung closely to the *exuvia.* He stood there, swaying in the breeze. He wondered what had happened to his body, it seemed so sleek and slender. As the aching subsided, he noticed a new sensation in his body: his shoulders did not feel the same, in fact, they seemed to be practically lifting off his body.

He looked, and saw there fine, transparent wings protruding from his shoulders and folded the length of his body. As he watched, he was amazed to see them slowly unfold at right angles to his body, four of them, dazzling in the light. In appearance, they were divided into a complex network of tiny diaphanous segments. They were glistening with a liquid that even now was beginning to evaporate in the sun's rays.

The cocoon was attached to a reed growing out of a pond. He clung there contemplating all that had befallen him. What he could not understand, was how he had come to be here. He had a distinct memory of going to bed in a suburban house...

As he clutched the empty shell of an old body, something flew past him; it had the same wings as him, but the body was somehow different. Suddenly he was aware of something at the end of his body that seemed to spring to life. Without a second thought, he let go with all six legs and launched into the air after the strange, alluring creature.

He found himself to be lighter than air and his wings gently but speedily propelled him beyond the reed where he had been clinging. The wings, twinned, super swift, ultra-light, seemed to be able to move him without any conscious effort on his part. His eyes were steadily focussed on the strange creature looping ahead.

She skipped down to the pond and hovered centimetres above the surface of the water. He followed her down and stopped behind her and likewise hovered just above the water. It was like a mirror, and reflected every curve of her body. Then she took off again, and he followed as if connected by an invisible thread to her.

She flew back down to the surface of the water, hovering as before, and he followed her down, hovering a little closer this time. Then she swivelled her head towards him and he saw her mouth move, but with no sound. However, he received a clear message.

"*Bugger off!*" She flew off, but he remained.

He was aware of a great emptiness inside; he was ravenously hungry. He noticed again the mosquitoes flying above. He remembered the revulsion he used to feel from a sting in the arm and seeing a mosquito feeding on his blood. Now, he felt the anticipation of the hunt and something deeply primeval: blood lust.

He took off into the air and flew up amongst the gliding insects. He focussed on one in particular and began to give chase. The mosquito was zigzagging in the air and making sudden dives. It was taking evasive action. He remembered mosquitoes being incredibly swift and difficult to swat. But, with these eyes and these wings, the mosquito seemed incredibly sluggish.

He swiftly narrowed the distance between them until he was flying directly above the insect, mimicking every twist and turn in its flight. Then he reached out his legs and caught the mosquito as if in a basket and drew the hapless insect up to his head. Then he began feeding on it in mid-flight, till there was nothing left between his legs but some broken wings which floated away. He was satiated for the moment.

His stomach full, he glided on automatic pilot, musing on this strange new life. Then, the realization struck him forcefully. He had only a matter of months to live.

This would be his last summer ever.

The sun set behind a bank of cumulus clouds on the horizon. The edges of the clouds shone golden. Above, a splattering of white smudges turned golden and then red against a blue sky shading into darkness. The whole spectacle was reflected on the surface of the pond as he watched from his perch on a leaf.

"Perhaps this will all turn out to be a vivid dream", he said to himself as he drifted off to sleep.

The next morning he woke up again, still on the leaf. A sense of panic gripped him. Then another female flew past and he received a different message from her. She was receptive.

In an instant, he was off the leaf and flying after her. Soon, they were coupled and flying in tandem above the surface of the pond. He found they could communicate almost telepathically, and he put to her the question that was burning in his mind:

"What do you remember of your past life?"

She replied, "It was under the surface of the water, dark and murky, no wings and nothing to see."

"Why, what do you remember?"

There was nothing he could say...

When they had finished, they separated and she flew down to the water to lay her eggs. He continued flying without direction, musing on his fate.

He began to wonder if he was deluding himself. Can an insect delude itself? Did he still remember going to bed in a suburban house? The memory was becoming hazy. This insect brain was not designed for names and dates. Oh no! What was his name? This brain was designed for navigating at ultra-swift motion in three dimensions, for spotting prey and for rapid pursuit. Not for names and dates. What was his birthday? All he could think of was coming out of that cocoon. He began to wonder if he even cared. The warm sun on his wings and body felt so good. Perhaps that was good enough for him. Enjoy life while you can. Seize the day! Or, seize the prey. He chuckled inwardly. Can an insect laugh at itself?

As he flew near the bank, he noticed two humans sitting on the grass there. He flew in closer and was shocked to recognise one of them as his wife.

"...a heart attack in the night, and just like that, he was gone."

She brushed away a tear as her friend held her other hand.

He flew in close to her face, desperately trying to communicate one thought to her mind.

She started back and shooed him away with her hand.

"Get away from me!" she screamed.

Bewildered, he retreated back over the pond. All his attention was focussed on the woman on the bank. How could he break through to her?

Suddenly, he was in shadow. He looked up. The last thing he saw was the wide open beak of a magpie diving at full speed upon him.

Anne Hanson

Anne's poetry has been published in several anthologies but those that appear in this one are new. A member of Tea Tree Gully Library Writers Group from 2013 Anne is passionate about the place of writing in recovery and health. She is both contributor and illustrator of *Women Alive! – Images of Healing* published in 2004. She is grateful for the encouragement and support of group members who generously share their talents and skills.

For Kathryn
by Anne Hanson

That day, when hunger was forgotten
river reeds waved their welcome
greeted like a long lost friend and
waited for the quiet to be filled.

That day, when eyes turned in
armour dissolved like a thief stealing anxiety
transporting to that place where
nothing is old and everything is new.

That day, when soft winds breathed
the earth shared stories
stories, that break through skin
giving light to darkened rooms.

That day, when birds filled the sky with raucous cries
shadows moved in lengthened grass
butterflies hovered over potholes of hope and
the sun simply shone.

Homeless
by Anne Hanson

Faceless people
living on nameless streets
where eyes look away
and loss leans like a tree
struck by lightning.

Sleepwalking silhouettes
heart heavy to hear
distance grows
staring through windows
at empty sunlight.

Frameless photos
cardboard boxes of memory
as drought shadows the night
voices sing within
like an ancient hymn.

Rapture
by Anne Hanson

I have known you
discovered you without a compass
traced the shape of your body
felt the passion pour from your lips
each kiss with you is like the first
each embrace wraps me in a
blanket of lost warmth
our bodies, tangled like seaweed.

Spending time with you
sends my senses brimming
only you have a way of
speaking the unspeakable
sparking conversations and convolutions.

You were at times a safe harbour
and also an obsession
throwing out paradoxes
where I, lost in meaning
both remember and forget.

Together
we have carved out a riverbed
entertained endless entities
built bridges to unfolding worlds
where each day is a new beginning
you cut shape into time
gratitude, for pens that pulse
heart beat ink.

Toy Boy – *SHAKESPEEEERING*
by Anne Hanson

Toy boy or not to toy boy
that is the question
though really, is much ado about nothing
since, tis nobler to suffer the slings
and arrows of jealousy than to miss out
on young men's love.

For age, it doth not wither her
even though rough winds do shake
the darling buds of may
a woman still looketh
like an innocent flower,
her beauty seduces men.

Friends, Romans, Countrymen
lend me your loins
tis a consummation devoutly to be wished
come, accelerate the pulse
for this is what dreams are made of
Oh Romeo, wherefore art thou?

Betty Artis

Betty alternates from heartfelt to horror with a few stops in between.

Her writing is personal and also fanciful. She enjoys exploring both the dark and light sides of life.

The Manor

by Betty Artis

'I'm out, I'm out!' This is my mantra as I flee in horror. My foot is shaking on the accelerator but I keep pressing down. I'm still on the driveway but the gates are getting closer. I'm through. Now the road. The more distance I can put between me and that house... I thought I was losing my mind but no...ghosts and demons are real! I can see a sign coming up for a town. Soon, I'll be back among people, amongst the living and this nightmare will end.

I had always wanted to stay in some gothic and romantic hideaway. Robert, a rich friend, lived in the English countryside; one of those perfect shires you might see on 'Escape to the Country'. I was between gigs which meant I had no meaningful employment, no meaningful relationship and a bit of saved cash to travel. England is the place to be if you want to at least fulfil the dream of looking like an invested writer. After I was invited, I quickly had my bags packed, tickets purchased and a few ideas bouncing around in my head. I landed at Gatwick Airport and was ferried by limousine, no less, to my new home for the next two months.

I was a bit surprised when I arrived at my destination when no one came out to greet me. My friend was going away for roughly the same amount of time that I planned to stay but I still thought he'd be here to welcome me. The driver must have seen my confusion.

'Mr. Hutson had to leave earlier than expected. He has left you a note on the hall table. He did ask me to pass along his regret that he wouldn't be able to spend time with you on your arrival but he did say that he would be back in about six weeks. Mr. Hutson said for you to make yourself at home. There's plenty of food and wood. The housekeeper will be back tomorrow morning.'

I felt awkward as the driver opened the main doors for me, turned on the lights, showed me where the note was left, dropped my suitcases off and then mumbled something about leaving before it got dark.

I wanted privacy and a bit of peace. The house, or really a manor, was huge. I picked up the note from the table and immediately felt dwarfed as I proceeded into the reception area of what could have been a grand hotel. There was a warm glow from the hundreds of prisms sparkling from the chandelier. A massive and detailed tapestry hung on one wall, landscape paintings on others, valuable antiques on heavy wooden furniture. I felt overwhelmed and afraid to touch anything. I picked my steps carefully absorbed in my vintage surroundings.

'Leave.'

'Who said that?' I blurted before I realised I should be alone.

'Leave!' More urgent this time but unmistakeable. 'Who's there?' Nothing.

I suddenly felt tired. Taking into account the hours in the air and the extra hours travelling to this remote location, I had every reason to nap. I thought about the jet lag factor but knew I couldn't stay awake. That's why I must be hearing things. There looked like a big comfy couch in the sitting room just off to the left. It was calling me. I turned on a desk lamp and a soft warm light filled the little corner. Dropping down into the well-worn upholstery, I quickly nodded off.

'LEAVE!'

My breath caught and I choked wondering for a moment where I was. England, manor house, big old couch. I felt cold and realised that I hadn't started a fire before dozing. Must have been the cold that stirred me so suddenly.

'LEAVE BEFORE IT'S TOO LATE!'

This time I knew what I heard. There is someone here.

I stood up and looked around for the room light and flicked the switch. No one.

'Hey Robert! You didn't leave at all, did you? Okay, okay, funny. Scare the tourist. Come out and you can light the damn fire.' No response.

I felt sure it must have been Rob playing a silly trick. Venturing out from the sitting room, I walked back into the main entry. The stairs swirled upward in a flourish but I did not feel comfortable walking into the unknown until I worked out where this mystery voice was coming from.

I don't scare easily so I thought logically instead. Robert could still be lurking somewhere waiting to pop out at a time he chose or maybe some kids from the village were playing with me.

'Leave before it's too late.'

Softer this time but still firm. There didn't seem to be an origin for the voice. It was here but then it was over there as though it were reverberating around the room. Voices come from people. What do the words mean though and who's speaking?

I started to take the first step up the grand staircase when 'LEAVE' shouted at me. An oily whisper breathed into my ear 'before it's too late!'

Crap! I called out, 'Okay. Enough! I'm scared, alright? There you've won. Now show yourself and let's get this over with.'

The tapestry flapped behind me. Something powerful had to lift that heavy fabric. The draught it stirred chilled me further. I felt frozen on that first step. Up or down? A standing lamp at the top of the landing rocked and crashed to the floor. 'LEAVE!' I waited. A book from a nearby bookcase flew at me. I ducked just in time. 'BEFORE IT'S TOO LATE!'

Cowering on the floor, I realised that I still had Robert's letter in my hand. I ripped it open, hoping for some clue. Skimming the waffle at the top, I zeroed in on the word 'car'. I was welcome to 'use the late model Rover; the keys are in the garage'. That's all I needed to know.

'LEAVE BEFORE IT'S TOO LATE!' It screamed.

'OKAY' I screamed back. 'I can take a hint! I'm gone.'

I ran out the front door leaving my bags behind and turned to where I had seen a large outbuilding on the drive up. It looked like a garage. Running hard I fell into the door then ripped it open. I stretched out my hand for the light, found a chain and pulled. The car was there as promised and the keys were on the ledge. I fumbled but was soon in the Rover and gunning the engine lowering the window as I passed the house. Rumbling through the corridors was the phrase, 'LEAVE BEFORE IT'S TOO LATE' over and over. I pressed the button closing the window never wanting to hear those words again.

I'm still on the driveway but the gates are getting closer. I'm through. Now the road. I can see a sign coming up for a town. Soon there'll be people... The awful screaming is left at the manor and I can slow the car for a bit. The house is miles behind me now.

The steering wheel is wrenched from my hand and twisted to full lock. I am now pointed toward an enormous oak tree.

I got out! I don't understand.

'Too late!'

The Vice

by Betty Artis

The man looked at the project. He hadn't been able to pick up the next piece of wood to turn for months now. He knew he needed to finish but the desire was not there. Inside him was a huge ball of knotted barbed wire. He didn't know how to unravel all the tangled barbs to free himself.

A few weeks later, he looked at the pieces of wood again. Maybe now. He told himself to make a start. His grief counsellor had suggested taking every part of the day mindfully. How he hated the new age sound of mindfulness. However, it did make sense. Small parcels of the day to unwrap. Never getting too far ahead of yourself. Living in the moment.

He inserted a table leg size piece of timber into the chuck of the lathe. His tools were to the side. He picked up the facing tool and clipped it into the holder. He leant over to the left of the machine and switched the power on. The repetition of the sound reassured him like a favourite song. He lowered the tool holder and felt the power return to his hands as the facing tool began to smooth out the corners and round what was square. He watched the smoothness unfold before his eyes. A small notch of pain unhinged from his shoulders. He realised how tense he had been. The machine came to a stop and he ran his right hand along the new surface.

The man switched tools now to the fillet. He wanted to smooth things out and begin the design. His muscles were warming up and he could feel the tingle of a small bead of sweat at his temple. He didn't wipe it away. He wanted to feel every sensation. He needed to be a splinter in the wood. Right now, in this moment, he wanted to be an oiled part of the machinery; to dissolve into creation. Forty minutes passed before he became aware of time again. He checked his watch as the wheel of the lathe slowed. He looked at his work and marvelled at the intricacies of the turned leg. This was the best work he had ever done. The design was alive in its clarity. The edges were sharp yet the curves were fluid.

He loosened the vice and replaced the completed leg with a new piece of wood. He decided to let the process happen without undue cluttered thinking. He started the lathe again and indulged in the freedom of his work. Again, time spun by until he woke from his trance. Just like before, the leg was stunning and vital. He could have felt the timber's pulse.

Removing the second leg, he ran his fingers down the smooth surface. He was at her hospital bed and stroking her long and slender arm. The smallest flicker of a smile ran over her face and fluttered over her lips. She never opened her eyes again. That was when the coil of barbed wire slithered and twined around his heart. He was not going to feel again. It was an agony that he had no use for and would not entertain. She was leaving him and he was powerless. He loved her beyond reason or words and no showing of grief would ever be enough. From that time, he switched off. He was like his lathe. No movement; just gathering cobwebs.

Until this quiet moment in his workshop. He had built many pieces of furniture but this was her dining suite. The one that she had been waiting for; waiting for him to retire so he could devote his time finally on something special for her. He felt the guilt clawing at his muscles as he pushed himself to go on. He had been selfish; fishing with his buddies and going off for drinks with those same friends. He never saw her sickness until it had moved in as a permanent member of the family. His wife had always smiled and told him to go off and play with his friends in that good natured way of hers. She never complained but sometimes he could feel her disappointment. Yet, it was never quite enough to put her first.

Now was too late. He could only hope that she would still see the finished project from somewhere and know that he really had loved her and hated her being gone. He wanted more time with her. He needed to feel her one last time.

A sudden gust bustled through the shed and settled on his cheek. He felt warm and held. His breath rasped and he felt tears roll down his face. He tried to choke back the sob but there was no holding back the weeping. He wept as the coil of barbed wire release its hold on his heart and the vice shattered as it fell to the floor.

Dark Humour
by Betty Artis

She coughed but there was something in her mouth causing her to splutter instead. Groggy and clouded in her head, she knew that she was restricted somehow. With a growing panic, she began to open her eyes. A few patches of light spread to where she was lying. If she stretched her neck to the left she should just make out a single bulb hanging from the ceiling.

Her face was pressed to the floor forcing small flurries of dust to dance in time with her ragged breathing. She struggled against her restraints trying to make sense of where and why? Her wrists and feet were bound making her thrash wildly.

"Stop wrestling around down there!" an unknown voice said. Where did it come from? She tried to look up but with her belly on the floor and her hands tied behind her, it was impossible.

"I'm up here on the bed. It'd be to your right. If you force your tongue out you might be able to loosen the gag."

For several minutes, Lucy manipulated her teeth and tongue to manoeuvre the cloth. Finally, she could feel some freedom and the gag rested on her chin. Coughing again, she asked,

"What's going on? Why are we here?"

"Aaah, the money question. We don't know and we don't know."

"We?"

"Oh yeah, there's two of us besides you."

"How long?"

"You've been here...?

"Lucy."

"Well, Lucy, what I think would be all night if I could see the sky, or outside. Hard to tell for me and Rachel, I think I've been here a couple of weeks. It's been longer for Rach."

Another voice joined in, "Welcome to Hell."

"So if you're Rachel, what's your name?"

"I'm Sophie. What do you remember?"

Lucy thought. Her head felt like it was clearing but she was still fuzzy on details.

"I know I was at work yesterday. Went out for a few drinks with the girls from work. Then..."

"Don't worry. We're pretty much the same" Rachel replied. "I was at a bar too."

"Me too," said Sophie. "Puts you off drinking forever."

Lucy had a thought. One that panicked her all over again. "On the news. They've been talking about women who've gone missing. One person survived though so the police think she was held by a serial killer. She's been on all the talk shows. She says that he plays laughter when he does stuff. I didn't know what she meant but the stupid media have dubbed him 'The Comedian'.

"Shit! He does do that!"

Suddenly the room was quiet like it too was held hostage.

After interminable minutes, Rachel offered, "Does it really matter what he does or what the press call him? We're going to die if we can't get out."

Lucy's voice felt small as she asked, "Has he...?"

"Yep. But it's better if you don't think about that. Why else would some psycho bastard kidnap young women? It's not for a friggin' chat!" Rachel snapped. "I'm sorry. You're new. It's got nothing to do with you. I can't rant at him right now."

Lucy felt that she was in the presence of extreme bravery. "God, if I'd been here as long as you...I don't know what I would be like. Jesus, these things happen to people in the movies not to people like us."

Sophie said in a frighteningly calm tone, "This isn't a film. We're not leaving. This is it for us. There's no cavalry on the way. We're not going to be saved at the last minute. He's had Rachel and me. Next, it's going to be you. How long before he decides that he's bored with his 'playthings'? He wants new and shinier. He's been doing this a long time and never been caught. He's too practised at this to be a novice. People get dumped all the time; at the side of a road, in a shallow grave, in a pit...who knows where half of them were before dying?"

Lucy jumped in. "Hey, the news said that the police were onto some leads. Maybe they know more than they're saying and they're close to finding him. We can't give up!"

"You are so new," Rachel said.

After a few minutes, Lucy spoke again. "What did that woman mean about the laughter?"

Sophie resettled herself on the wire bed frame causing it to creak loudly. This jangled Lucy's nerves even further and she shuddered.

"Please. I need to know."

"You don't, but I'll tell you anyway. He likes to tell jokes", the bed shook again as this time Sophie shuddered. "He has a recorded laugh track on constantly. The more excited he gets the faster he tells them and the faster the laugh track runs. He seems to have it all timed to perfection. It's so sick! He takes something joyful and fucks with it! I never thought I could hate the sound of laughter so much."

Another long silence as the three women were lost in their own thoughts and memories. Lucy was the first to speak, "How long do I have? Before he comes for me?"

"I wish I could say that you had days to process all of this but he'll be here soon. Actually, I thought he would have been here well before now. He 'loves us' when we're a 'fresh audience'. Rachel? Isn't he usually quicker than this?"

"Yeah. I wonder what's happening to him. Hope he's lying in a gutter somewhere or someone's decided to ream him!"

A pause. Lucy spoke, "But if something happens to him, we'll never be found!"

A longer pause this time as they realised that dying of thirst wouldn't be a whole lot better.

No words needed. They each were locked in their own fears. Rushed movement upstairs.

"He's here. What's happening? This is different."

They each strained to listen to the thunderous noise from above. Furniture seemed to be moved. Something fragile must have shattered on the floor. Dragging sounds of heavy items being shifted. Something high pitched in the distance. Too many sounds.

"Hang on" said Sophie, 'is that sirens?

Far away but getting closer.

"They've found him. Found us. We're going to be okay. I knew it! I knew it!" Lucy screamed.

Something began to pour in from the floor vents of the basement room. First a tickle at the back of the throat then a choked laugh. Sirens were definitely getting closer though so the women began to relax. A slightly sweet odour began to fill their nostrils and they all laughed. It seemed like all the build-up of tensions releasing at once. They laughed more. Suddenly, the laughter seemed forced.

"Why are we laughing?" Lucy said.

"We're going to get out. That's why" Rachel replied.

"No, seriously," spluttered Sophie amid the giggles. "Why are we laughing?"

They all felt mildly relaxed yet couldn't stop laughing. If they could have seen each other they would have seen a wild panic in each other's eyes. The laughter continued. The sirens were louder now.

Movement came from upstairs again, the door of the cellar was flung open and light spilled down the steps as rapid footsteps kept in pace.

"Time, Ladies!" A smoother than expected voice said. "This is it. This is where you will be found. Shame you won't be alive when the police heroically break through the barricade but can't have witnesses."

"You're probably wondering why I'm not as cheerfully cackling as you lot. I've gotten used to Nitrous Oxide over the years, being a dentist and all. And yes, if you've a bit of chemistry knowledge...yep, it's laughing gas!"

"It's been fun but it's time to move on. Always is. Love to spend more time finishing this but time is of the essence. You'll all be glad to know that this will be quick."

He moved to Rachel, her body shaking with laughter, pulled her head up by her hair, drew his knife and slit her throat. Blood gushed as she gurgled. He moved on. Methodically, he did the same with Sophie and then finally he reached Lucy. He took the time to wipe away her tears as he cupped her face in his hand. Her body still wracked with laughter though her eyes shone with terror. "It would have been fun" were the last words she heard as the blade sliced through her jugular.

The sirens were extremely close now as the first responders reached the scene. He knew he had just enough time to escape. He'd done this so many times before.

He left the grisly scene behind knowing that they had all died laughing.

Feckless Folk
by Betty Artis

He never had to struggle
Or fight for what he had
Never answered consequences
Bailed out by Mum and Dad

She's taking another selfie
Another duck face for her page
Rarely sees around her screen
Snapchat is God and sage

Temper tantrums of an infant
Are indulged and placated
Mollycoddled and disabled
Responsibility vacated

Bullying to murder
Ripping others to pieces
Compassion dies friendless
Loneliness increases

Parents throwing money
Instead of spending time
Leaving children unattended
Then cry when there's a crime

When we think of ourselves
As the only game in town
We flood ourselves with hubris
We sink and then we drown

Don Warren

Don has been in the Group for eight years. A registered pharmacist for 57 years, also studied and taught theology and served as a pastor and hospital chaplain. A co-founder of a significant faith-based school; a cross-cultural worker in Papua New Guinea and for short periods in the Solomon Islands, the Ukraine and the Middle East.

Adelaidians, Jean and Don lived for four years in England where two of their four children were born. His writing shows deep thought and lively ideas.

Faringdon, Here We Come

by Don Warren

We had met Millie when she came to Adelaide. She came to spend time with her son, his wife and two grandchildren. We got to know Millie and being the hospitable person she was we were invited to stay in her house in Faringdon in England. We said, "thank you," and filed this thought away in our minds. We also knew a couple who now lived in Bandung in Indonesia. They had also said come and visit us.

Our final destination was Cyprus at this time, and we had to go through London to get there. So we thought, yes we can stay with our friends in Bandung and then with Millie in England before flying to Cyprus. We had a great three weeks in Bandung, also visiting Jakarta, Bogor and Cirebon. In Jakarta we went to court because our friend had committed a traffic offence. It was that he was so excited when we arrived in Jakarta that he drove the wrong way down a one-way street. He refused to pay the police officer the requested bribe so had to face the judge. In Bogor we got up close and personal with the Komodo dragon. He even allowed us into his enclosure. In Cirebon we admired the historic Dutch architecture and feasted at McDonalds. Travel back to Jakarta was by comfortable train. At the airport they said, 'Upgraded to Business Class for you', for the flight to Singapore.

At Singapore an urgent situation arose and only squat toilets were free. Squatting with a rush when there is great urgency results in disaster. Much cleaning up, both personal, clothes and the floor was the result. We dozed as we waited for our very late flight out of Singapore to Heathrow. With our long flight ahead we reflected that already we had been in travel mode since early morning.

An uneventful flight saw us on time descending into Heathrow. Yes, there was fog at Heathrow, but it was lifting. Then everything changed. Fog came down again and we went suddenly up and were now on our way to Amsterdam.

Five hours later after nothing to eat and only water to drink we took off for England to loud cheers from all the passengers. Even then there was uncertainty just where we would land. Would it be Manchester or Heathrow? Everyone was glad that the fog had cleared and Heathrow it was to be. And thankfully, for that was where many of us were being met by our friends.

Millie had come early and waited all those hours. She had been driven there by her nephew whilst his wife had driven their car to be able to take him back home. Millie had a broken arm and could not drive. But that was all right. After travelling from early morning in Bandung we would drive all the way back to Millie's house in Faringdon.

I knew something of what lay ahead. I was to drive us from the morass of Heathrow roads out onto the dreaded M25 circle road to get us headed north. We found ourselves heading in the correct direction, so essential, and at high speed. Naturally there were the frequent slowdowns and stoppages until at last we found the correct exit to take us north. How relieved I was at that point.

But we were not there yet. On we went until at last we were on the road leading into the town of Faringdon. As we pulled up, Millie assured us she had a special lunch waiting for us. Now what do you think we had been living on in Indonesia? For carbohydrate we ate rice and for protein, chicken. Now our treat was to be revealed to us. You will guess what it was.

Dear Millie, she was so kind and generous. We often had the house to ourselves as she had a voluntary job which meant she stayed away overnight. She had also bought a car for our use whilst we stayed with her. We had a great time in historic Faringdon and surrounds until we flew away to Cyprus, visiting Middle East countries and staying there till the end of that eventful year.

Jill Wherry

Jill Wherry was born in Northern Ireland. She married in the early 1960s, immigrated to Australia, resumed a busy teaching career and reared a family. Now retired, Jill has time to pursue her interest in poetry and records the quirky side of her life's experiences through verse.

In 2009 Jill published 57 of her original comic poems in 'Definitely not Shakespeare' and in 2015 she published her second book '40 Reasons to Smile'. Jill has also produced two CDs.

Many of Jill's poems have been published. She has won prizes in the NE Writers Poetry Festival, Salisbury Poetry festival and Bush Poets Festivals.

Jill soon branched into performance poetry and in 2005 won the SA Bush Poets Performance Championships.

Since then she has twice reached the finals of the SA Poetry Slam and has performed with a U3A group in two Fringe shows. Jill has been interviewed and has recited her poetry on three local radio stations, including 891AM with Peter Goers.

She enjoys the role of MC at Bush Poetry and Pub Poetry events. Jill continues to travel around Adelaide and nearby towns entertaining social groups and providing light-hearted, humorous entertainment.

Letter to an Ex
by Jill Wherry

Are the photos you once treasured not around you anymore?
Did you take our smiling memories and stuff them in a
drawer?
Or perhaps they've been recycled deep inside a darkened
bin.
While her photos have a special place among your next of
kin.
When she's serving up your dinner, does she know it can't be
late?
Does your Milo keep appearing at exactly half past eight?
When she's picking out a special shirt she's hoping you will
wear,
Is it one that I have purchased and selected with great care?
When you're working in her garden and you swelter in the
heat,
Will she offer you iced water and occasionally a treat?
Does she purchase trendy sporting gear so you can dress in
style?
Does she seek out hard Sudukos in the hope they'll make you
smile?
When you're watching games of footy, sev'ral matches in a
row,
Will she hang around quite happily and not pack up and go?
Does she share your love of Pokies? Didn't we have fun with
those?
I expect she is too sensible, a pity I suppose.
Was she ever so delighted when your family came to tea?
I sincerely hope they liked her, but not quite as much as me.
Does she dare turn up the music when she hears her
favourite song,

Or leave dirty dishes soaking though you've let her know it's wrong?
Does she grieve about the falling shares that so affect your wealth?
Can she handle all the drama with your fluctuating health?
For your birthday celebrations, will she write a special verse?
Has she thought about her future and perhaps a role as nurse?
Do her grand-kids need a grand-dad or have they already two?
You became the only grand-pa my son's children ever knew.
Does she share in your opinions and do everything she's told,
Or be daringly defiant and deserves to hear you scold?
Can she calm you down successfully when you grow really cross?
Is she always in agreement when reminded who's the boss?
When there's never an apology and rarely any praise,
Will she realise the 'honeymoon' was just a passing phase?
If eventually she's had enough and speaks out firm and strong,
Why on earth should you apologize when you are never wrong?
When you open up this email, such confronting truths you'll meet.
But you can't erase these mem'ries just because you press delete.

Mobile Blues
by Jill Wherry

For years I have been proud to own
My pride and joy, a mobile phone.
But sadly here's the latest news,
I'm suffering from mobile blues.
Last week I was a wedding guest.
We all took photos; mine were best!
My son said, 'Mum' and gave a groan.
'You have no data on your phone.'

'Your Facebook friends would love to share
The smiling guests who've gathered there.'
He takes my phone, it works out fine
And soon my photos are on line.

But what a shock what happens next.
In comes a most disturbing text.
One that makes me want to holler.
Telstra's charged me twenty dollar.

No more feelings of elation.
Life is full of consternation.
I ring my son, 'Please tell me how.
I must remove the data now.'

When he instructs me what to do,
I follow his directions through.
But Telstra isn't happy still.
Forty dollars now my bill.

Glimpses 3

I ring up Telstra but you see
A robot tries to answer me.
It can't translate and that's a shame.
I fear my accent is to blame.

At last I manage to get through,
Explain myself to one then two.
But both of them are Mr Wrong.
Now number three has joined the throng.

I cry and tell him what's the matter.
He waives the fee takes off the data.
But Murphy's Law strikes all the time.
Next morning I am still on line.

So all my daily tasks I drop.
I storm up to the Telstra shop
And tell my story as you do.
I'm passed along to someone new.

By now I'm growing quite insane.
How many times must I explain?
At last someone who's in the know
Makes all that pesky data go.

She goes on line, locates my bill.
With forty dollars lurking still.
She says, 'I've waived the fee for you.'
Oh how I hope her words are true.

For happy ending, waiting still
Won't know until I get the bill
But nevermore, you'll hear me groan.
For these days, I'm with VODAPHONE!

Pillow Talk
by Jill Wherry

I have a special pillow and I've shared it with a few
I lead a single's lifestyle now so what's a girl to do?
Life changes so completely when you're back upon the shelf.
And is it even pillow talk, when chatting to yourself?
A pillow, or a special man, I wonder which is best.
Which one will help me realise I'm well and truly blessed?
With pillows you can snuggle till the dawn of morning light
But men may leave on tip-toe when you're fast asleep at
night.
A partner waters gardens and a partner cuts the grass.
Your pillow's just a useless lump and can't get off its ass.
A bloke is often grumpy and will swear and snore and frown.
Your pillow always props you up and never puts you down.
Smart partners fix computers, they are experts in I.T.
My pillow doesn't have a brain and can't converse with me.
My pillow's always by my side no matter what I do
While men, are prone to cheating and acquiring someone
new.
Your pillow's never jealous even though you own another
But girls, a man is vital if you yearn to be a Mother.
A bloke, if he is disciplined, is likely to escape.
It's better with a pillow; you can punch it into shape.
Deciding is impossible but I know what to do.
I'll buy an extra pillow, find a bloke - or maybe two!

Maureen Mitson

Maureen is the author of a well-received South Australian historical trilogy, a popular YAL novel about the pre-techno age, a memoir and many quirky short stories which have been read over radio. An occasional poet, she leads a poetry group at the TTG U3A, is included in a number of wide-ranging anthologies and enjoys speaking publicly about her varied writing and life-style experiences.

The Chocolate Cake – a riddle.
by Maureen Mitson

My first in *delectable*, also in *lick,*
my second in *thinner* and also in *thick.*
My next is in *oven* and *glove* if it's hot,
my fourth is in *creamy,* and lumpy it's not.
My next in *delicious* but never in taste,
another in *spoonful* but never in paste.
My next is in *balance* and also in *beat,*
my next in *thermometer* testing for heat.
My ninth is in *mixture* and *egg;* not in yolk;
my tenth in *creative*, the talent of folk.
My next is in *sugar* but never in mix
My twelfth is in *tricky* and never in fix.
My last is in *pleasure, success* and in *feat;*
the whole a delectable, lip-smacking treat!

First printed in the NSW Education Magazine

Rocking Horse
by Maureen Mitson

The vice stands on the workman's bench, its mission to connect.
Solid, sound, well oiled and greased, no victim of neglect.
He calls upon it to respond to all his loving care
each nut and bolt and cog and wheel is waiting, weight to bear.

He clamps the boards and layers the glue, the timbers strictly level;
each layer horizontal with no vestige of a bevel,
thicknesses consistent, correlating with the gauge
with alignments equidistant and the grain a mark of age.

No warp upon these timbers that he treats with such respect.
The vice? Its jaws are cladded so no punctures will deflect
from Grandad's planned perfection for this very special toy,
this rocking horse a joy to make, to give a favoured boy.

The metal struts are well aligned, the vice has had them clamped
The horse's head and face are glued, their features finely stamped.
The saddle has been padded; leather moulded on a cast,
its buttons well cemented by adhesives made to last.

The stirrups have been welded on to swivel from the saddle
their fastenings secured because the youngsters climb to straddle.
The face and body varnished, he plaits the tail and mane
and Grandad ponders as he weaves; will he do all this again?

Tea-Totalled

by Maureen Mitson

Heading for her century and known for her sweet smile and tortoiseshell combs, Elisabetta epitomised the gracious great-grandmother. I'd visit as often as I could and out would come the Johnson stoneware teapot with the blue flowers on and the spicy *pfefferkuchen.*

'Don't you find it inconvenient, All those little bits of burnt leaf blocking the spout of your pot?'

'Why, Elena. Do you find it awkward to drink, unpleasant to the tongue?'

I felt abashed. 'No, I don't, in fact the taste is exquisite; reviving and with a hint of a holiday campfire about it... tempting images, Granny Lisa.'

She laughed – her hearty, bell like peal ringing around the room. Her budgie squawked in his cage *'Cuppa tea only the best! Cuppa tea only the best'!*

'Elena – you have taste. This tea is traditionally smoked over pine bark drawn from a certain Chinese province. It's Lapsang Souchong. Some don't like the flavour; some prefer the orange bergamot in the Earl Grey. Each to her own, I say. I know I can sip my pot slowly and it retains flavour even when it cools down. When I'm knitting, sitting in my window watching the world go by, when no-one comes to call, it is no less enjoyable a drink than now. Tea is always my choice.'

'When I think of you Granny Lisa, it is as you are now; warm woolly cardie against the draughts and your silvery-gold hair tied up and back with that tortoiseshell comb; sitting back against your big cushions, your knitting needles and yarn ready – and to hand. That's my picture of you, a gentlewoman of the old school, just being gentle! I'm sure you deserve the leisure after your years at the library. I hope I'm as lucky as you when I am older. Though I think the world comes to you rather than you simply watching it go by your window.'

She turned to look at me, eyebrows raised in query. 'I have been lucky, Elena?' She smiled, rather a strange sad-happy one. 'I guess luck did come into it but....'

'Dear Granny Lisa. Look here. I collected your post as I came in. For most older people the mail is stamped Centrelink. These few are from'... I sifted through the pile of envelopes, 'the German embassy, the Governor General –goodness me – the Passport Office and the Refugees Association. Among others. Intriguing. See what I mean?'

She took from me the Governor General's envelope, slit it open, turned to the light from the window and started to read. It seemed as if minutes flew by, then she held it out to me to read. 'Leisure has to be earned my dear Elena. It seems some people feel I have done just that.'

This first letter was advising her of an award to be bestowed on the Queen's Birthday List. To anyone looking in that window I would have appeared wide-eyed, open-mouthed and quite simple minded. I wanted to ask what was in her mind but she was gazing – in that unfocused way some day-dreamers adopt – at something, somewhere, beyond my knowing. The budgie tucked his head under his wing. A blowfly was buzzing. Somewhere. I decided to wait.

Then she spoke. I sensed the effort she made in wrestling the words from deep inside.

'Elena, I'm sorry. Just noticed the date on the letter. Memory is itself a construction, particularly as it becomes in time distanced from actual events. Mark Twain said that and it stayed with me but well I remember this date. It was in 'forty-four, I was based in UK, flying with the Air Transport Auxiliary to France. I'd flown up north, in the Daly River country, from when I was fourteen; cattle. Our station had cruel terrain, flight was the way to go, so we did. I had an English side to the family and he heard of my ability and asked me to sign up. I did in '42. Our ATA delivered planes every day either straight from the factory or overhauled, painted in camouflage or roundels to wherever we were told. Our favourites were the Spitfires, real fighters; we flew them from the factories near Hamble to just about every airbase in southern England. My last flight was Hastings; it was before the invasion proper began and I was warned to watch for flying bombs – called the Vee Ones. Plenty in the sky those weeks and hard to spot. They were the only real enemy for we ATA pilots because we were civilians and as such, no weaponry permitted. Bomb bays stayed empty, gunsights disconnected, we didn't dog fight. Nor did we have radios. No maps that would give away positions. We really felt on our own at times up there. Enemy had their equivalent mob too and we all relied upon that honour that existed among pilots, even enemy fighters, to let us through. Like a gentlemen's agreement. Usually worked.

'But deflecting a V1 was our game, we would try to flick them a wing tip and deflect them from their target. Then could feel we'd done our bit. Our way of getting back at them... Then one day I was blown over the channel -no distance from Hastings – and spotted by a *Messerchmitt Me-262* in full *Luftwaffe* camo. He'd come in too close, wondered why. Realised he'd been setting the V1s. No gentleman this one! He waved the wings, shot high to scare me then started to herd me out into the channel, using the wind. Spits were lightweight. Couldn't lose my plane. Had to try and save it. We chased all over the skies, he didn't fire after all, probably expected I'd run out of fuel. I did run dry. Too soon I was shunted over the border into Normandy. Honour bound; had to land. Tried to remember German positions. Too late to worry. Downed, I clambered onto the wing and suddenly they were all around the plane. Clapping; hadn't expected a woman to fly a Spit. Hated Nazi uniforms. Damnation!

An officer barked. I was shunted into a truck, solid sides, dark. Only me, crates and a rough, soggy floor. We drove for hours. I was frozen! A sudden stop, the doors flung open and

I was pulled out, crashed onto a cindered road, took the skin off both knees. Hit my head. Woke up some time later to an attractive blonde woman with a scarred face asking me 'Vous êtes anglaise?'

'Australienne. Er... Ou est nous... erm, where is this place? You speak English?'

'Ravensbrück, a women's prison, in their language a *Konzentrationslager*. I am a Résistante. They move us place to place as Allies advance. 'Orrible women traitors, our guards.'

I had no words. Sitting here in Elisabetta's living room by her window, I was gobsmacked. The French resistance? She was sitting, unmoving, remembering. My ninety-nine year old great-grandma, a so-proper ex-librarian, was telling me... what? That her uneventful, sober-sides working life had been only a façade! I'd loved her and respected her all my life but *her* life, I had thought was, well, underwhelming; its only colour her knitting yarns. A flyer, pilot, prisoner of war - my Granny Lisa?

The budgie woke. His squawk broke the spell. '*Cuppa tea only the best'!* Granny Lisa inhaled, straightened her shoulders, and smiled sideways at me.. 'Sorry about that. One reason why I so enjoy my cups of tea; it was a rare drink for me at that time of my life. For a good few years in fact. Not until much later when I was I was able to help the Resistance girl escape. She's now an Aussie too. Not sure how much of all that qualifies as 'luck' though.'

Her smile widened. 'Now, how about another cup; perhaps a *leisurely* one?'

Credit to Elizabeth Wein: 'Rose Under Fire'.
www.egmont co.uk

Connie Berg

Connie is a writer, an editor, and a manuscript assessor. She is a teacher, a trainer, and a mentor to creative people. Her radio segment, 'Today's Writing Tip' has aired on PBA FM's *Words Out Loud* programme since 2014. She is co-Founder and Festival Organiser for the Langhorne Creek Writers' Festival. She founded and is Publisher and Editor for Sunshine Press, an independent, Print-On-Demand press which helps people self-publish.

Day Two: Kakopetria

by Connie Berg

We had talked of little else while checking into our room, showering, over dinner. We lay awake, and I whispered, 'We were so lucky.'

My husband continued our shared story, 'If we had kept going into the storm instead of going off the road where we did...'

I told the next part. 'Those switch backs, no guard rails, the cliffs.'

He sighed. 'The people here, their generosity.'

'All the offers. Help. Food. Water. Shelter. Amazing.'

Sumac

by Connie Berg

'Oh,' Annette exclaimed as they rounded the bend and the vibrant crimson foliage burst into view. 'The Sumac has begun to turn. Hello, autumn.' She sighed wistfully as they passed; she would need to pack up her summer dresses and dust off her box of knitted jumpers.

'*Rhus hirta*, or Staghorn Sumac. Derives its name from its thick, velvety upper branches, which resemble the antlers of young male deer.' John shifted down, then up through the gears to execute the hairpin turn with great skill. John relished in the mastery of things, including knowledge. Fortunately, his insatiable quest never approached boorishness, in fact, it was as boyishly charming as the grin he flashed at her.

Annette smiled and took up their familiar intellectual sparring. 'Native Americans ate the young shoots, the roots and the fruit raw. Some tribes believed that Sumac could foretell the weather and the changing of the seasons, so it was held as a sacred plant.' Annette saw the world though connections and viewpoints. She believed that viewing something through multiple perspectives was the key to seeing it fully.

'Mainly pollinated by bees and wasps, moths and butterflies eat the foliage,' John said whilst shifting. Another curve in the road brought a valley full of lipstick-red into view.

'According to the Muscogee Creek, the Horned Serpent is a snake that lives in the water and has horns like a stag. It has special powers, and it eats Sumac.' This earned Annette a nod of respect from John.

She continued, 'Its iridescent scales and the large crystal in its forehead were prized for their powers of divination.'

'Assuming you can catch one?'

Annette had to concede the point.

'However,' she quickly recovered, 'the bark and roots were used for all types of medicine, treating colds, fever, diarrhoea, and stomach aches. The blossoms made eye wash, leaves chewed for sore gums and lips, and the powdered bark made into a poultice to sooth a rash.'

'Like you would get from *Toxicodendron vernix*, or poison sumac, which causes skin and mucus membrane irritation on contact, and when burned and the smoke is inhaled, causes painful ulcerations in the lungs and respiratory difficulty which could be fatal.' John looked almost smug.

'But, that variety is only found in the Eastern US, in swampy areas, not like Staghorn.' Annette gestured out the window. 'Which is found in all US states and southern Canada in amongst the regular foliage. But not Alaska or Hawaii.'

'It goes by many different names,' John added, 'Dwarf Sumac, Mountain Sumac, Scarlet, Smooth, Shoemake, and many more.'

Annette hesitated, thinking, then said, 'Some people are naturally immune to the poisonous Sumac.'

John jumped on the chance. 'Not true! Whilst some people may not get an urushiol-induced rash at first, once you've been exposed, you become more sensitive and have a stronger allergic response the next time.'

Annette needed something extraordinary in order to stay in the game. She took a deep breath and recited:

The hem of her dress
hints just pink
and then a bright blush.
I think she is modest
knowing that soon
her Sumac skirt will drop
and bare her lovely legs
to the pale winter sun.

John was speechless, which was a rarity. 'Wow,' was all he managed. 'Who wrote that?'

Annette's lips curved up in pleasure. 'I did.'

Pauline Smith

Pauline has been a member of the Writers' Group for twenty-two years, and she loves the use of words and putting them into stories or poems.

In the late 1990s, Pauline was active in putting together two published books of stories and poems for a group she belonged to, and she found the experience challenging.

She is a Max Fatchen Poetry Competition winner and a contributing author to the Tea Tree Gully Library book *History of Tea Tree Gully*. She had a story included in the *Trail Of Tales* in 2016.

The Little Red Car
by Pauline Smith

They'd prayed for drought breaking rains
And cheered when floods crossed the plains
But the bridge was too far
For that little red car
When, with a thunderous frown,
Churning, muddy water pulled it down
Into the depths of its dark, unyielding hold
Leaving the mother and child to drown in the cold

Old Boots

by Pauline Smith

Strange how a casual remark can cause pain, but that's what happened when I overheard a high pitched woman's voice exclaim, 'Gee, those boots are old. They should have been thrown out years ago.'

I swear if I'd been closer I would have kicked her immaculate, shining black shoes. But then amusement curled at my toes. A sense of humour was something I'd developed many years ago.

'These boots,' announced my owner, affectionately stroking my right one, 'have been faithful friends of mine for many years. It would be very difficult to replace them.'

What she said was true and I was willing to admit it. I'd started off life as a pair of sturdy, no nonsense, tan-coloured walking boots. Not a wrinkle in my skin, tall and upright. But let's face reality, my life had fallen into the hands of a woman who loved to walk and I'd set out on the serious task of proving I could match her every need.

To coin a phrase, "I've had a very fortunate life." Not many boots could match my achievements. I've walked all the Heysen Trail, up rugged hills and down hills, battled through thick scrub, slithered through mud and icy waters. I've even been confronted by a wild bull, and I make no apology for being scared when I imagined his horns tearing at me, but now I can remember it with pride as we ran away and escaped. Once I thought a wombat wanted to eat me, but he was only being friendly. I've seen so much wildlife in the outback, from snakes, crocodiles, emus, kangaroos and so much more. It was quite an indignity when I fell into that cow pat, and all this thick dark stuff oozed over me. I don't think my owner appreciated the awful smell that stayed with me for a while.

I've been blessed with a very thoughtful owner, who has taken the time to lovingly clean and care for me. Three new pairs of sturdy laces have also been supplied. After all it is my job to provide support and comfort for my owner, no matter what she puts me through, and I know she's appreciated my loving concern for her welfare.

We've been to Coober Pedy together, but here I changed colour when we went noodling in the opal fields and both of us became covered in white dust. The deserts are always a challenge, hot and endless, but after the rains the flowers are beautiful to see and walk through. I don't like town and am always happy to escape to the next adventure.

Gradually after so many years of travel, I finally had to face the fact that I was getting past it. My tan faded to grey, my insides offer little support, I'm wrinkled and my bottoms are worn thin.

The words of that nasty woman must have given my owner something to think about as well, so it was no surprise when I saw the next generation of boots appear next to me on the veranda. They were tan, sleek, upright and very shiny. I'll make sure we have a chat together as I will be able to pass on some useful hints on how to look after my owner.

I feel sadness that my days of travel are over, but no one can take away the memories. I'm content to spend the rest of my life lounging on the veranda.

Moira McGee

Moira has been a member of the Group for several years. She has entered competitions and had one of her short stories published and paid for in an anthology. She enjoys writing short stories to a theme with the occasional poem thrown into the mix. Her ideas pop up from everywhere, even the odd dream! She is the Group's Treasurer plus tea, coffee and biscuit provider as the Group's creative juices require plentiful lubrication.

Flood

by Moira McGee

As I sit trembling in the unlit room the word 'flood' pops into my head. How useful is that word apart from its obvious meaning. Flooded by fear and adrenalin as I am now. Floods of tears, floods of anger, floods of praise, floods of pity, floods of guilt. I've experienced all of them at some time. Now I'm waiting for him to come, maybe even them. I know it will be tonight.

Why was I in the wrong place at the wrong time? Saw something I shouldn't have. If only I could go back to last week. Before it all happened. How wonderful if one could do that. Last week, although I didn't realise it then, I was carefree, happy even. Why do we always let the minutia of life spoil the present? Why can't we embrace the mundane? Appreciate it, expand into it? Right now I'd embrace mundanity.

Oh, was that a noise outside? Just a passing car.

Why is this happening to me? I mean I don't deserve this, I'm not a bad person. I don't think I am anyway. Perhaps I could have been less churlish and critical of my mother. Less snappish with my Dad when he became old and annoying. I'm quite honest though. Never stolen from anyone. Maybe didn't pay back a couple of people who'd loaned me money. Really, I don't think they expected it back anyway.

That was a noise, definitely.

Maybe I should pray. Get down on my knees, do it properly. Can't focus on anything, can't concentrate. I wonder who'll miss me. I mean, really miss me or will it just be an inconvenience for a few people, me not being around anymore. Colleagues at work trying to figure out where I've stopped so they can continue, evenly. My sister, but she's far away and has her own problems. Neighbours, no. Friends. They'll be shocked but not for long.

I wonder what being dead is like. Whether I'll go up or down. That is if there is an up or down. This waiting is awful. I'm beginning to feel hungry. A cup of tea and a biscuit? Oh stop it. Nothing matters now. I could have acquired a giant box of chocolates and gorged myself on them and to hell with the diet.

That's the doorbell. That can't be him. Why would he ring the doorbell? Its ring is insistent. I get to my feet and head down the hallway to open the door.

'Hello, it's me.'

'Yes, I've been expecting you. Come in, make it quick.

Matchbox

by Moira McGee

'Oh, why do old people hang on to so much junk? Zoe moaned before plumping down onto a chair. Her boyfriend Tyson laughed and said 'Well you offered to help your Mum and Dad clear out your Great- Gran's house.'

'So, why didn't you stop me?'

'Come on Zoe, you loved her and you have got through a lot this morning.'

'I know' Zoe sighed, 'but just take a look at this for instance.'

She held out a matchbox to show Tyson the contents. It wasn't the small type of matchbox you buy by the dozen but one that had contained long matches perhaps for lighting open fires and this box measured 13x7 cms. It held a tiny baby's yellowed bootee, a small charm depicting what could have been a goblin or pixie and a piece of paper with faded handwriting and the names Bob and Robert.

'What on earth is this all about, there are no Bobs or Roberts in our family.'

'We're never going to know the answer to that one Zoe, chuck it on that pile for the rubbish.'

No, they would never know the sadness that matchbox contained and the story behind its contents. An old but familiar story. At sixteen her Great-Gran. had had a sweetheart who was about to be sent to the front in 1915. They would have been married had they had a future. The dreaded telegram arrived to say missing presumed dead three short months later. The sweetheart was called Bob and the little charm was his leaving gift to her as he always called her 'his pixie.' Pixie discovered she was pregnant and in 1915 that was a shameful secret so she was sent away from home to a place for unmarried mothers. The girls there had to earn their keep and weren't treated very well by the nuns who ran the institution. It was a given that the child would be taken from the mother and adopted by a deserving couple.

Pixie had a miserable few months in the home and didn't want to part with her baby, a boy she named Robert, in her head of course. She wasn't given a choice but vowed to herself she would find him eventually, but she never did. So, twin sorrows to bear, the loss of both her future husband and their child. She had knitted several small garments for the baby and kept one bootee to remember him by, plus the charm together with their names. Life goes on and in her twenties Pixie married and had three more children but she never forgot Bob and Robert and no-one in her family ever mentioned what had happened. She never told her husband, it was her secret sorrow and went with her to the grave.

Zoe got up out of the chair still holding the matchbox. She'd felt a slight shiver as she'd held it.

'Let's do another hour of this then we can go for some lunch.'

'Great idea.'

'I don't think I'll chuck this in the rubbish just yet, I'm going to show it to Mum and see if she can make any sense of it.'

An hour or so later Zoe put the matchbox into her bag, grabbed Tyson's hand and they left. Just as the door closed a tiny sigh, like an exhalation of breath, eddied round the room.

The ID

by Moira McGee

Deena drew back her curtains to reveal a promise of sunny, windless weather. I'll forgo my usual, local walk and be more adventurous today, she decided, and I think I might just manage to enjoy retirement after all. Hmm, where to go. She filled a flask with coffee then remembered the new wetlands area she'd read about recently and not more than 10ks away. That's it. An hour later and she was walking there, occasionally stopping to examine a plant or read a nature notice. She sat down after a while to have coffee and revel in the peace. She hadn't met another soul. Deena's eyelids drooped and she gave in to a nap.

When she opened her eyes again someone was standing in front of her. She scrambled to her feet, caught off guard and even more confused when the apparition spoke.

"Hello, human person."

Fully awake, ready to run, she registered that her surroundings had subtly altered and the figure standing there was unusual. It was around her own height of 174cms, very thin, of indeterminate sex, with a disproportionately large, hairless head. It wore a narrow two-piece colourless linen ensemble and the face was expressionless.

"Come with me and bring your weapon."

Deena picked up her coffee flask and followed obediently. She didn't feel afraid and didn't even ask where they were going. They arrived at a large, cylindrical building without windows and an entry space suddenly sprang open. They stepped inside.

"You are my first specimen of the day."

Deena didn't care for the sound of that.

"Aren't you the same species as me?"

Her companion stopped and faced her.

"We are from another planet and have come to examine humans. We are curious as to how they function and we are going to examine you, outside and inside."

He, Deena thought of it as a he, led the way to an area set out as a laboratory where many 'people' were busy at benches. The stench was appalling and Deena saw that there were human body parts everywhere, being dissected. Huge containers were set around the perimeter of the area, all holding a human corpse. She gasped and recoiled in horror then stood rigidly upright, breathing shallowly.

"You seem to be a calm human," he observed, "others I've brought here have screamed and begged for their lives or run around in circles pummelling the walls seeking an exit. We won't hurt you, your expiry will be painless."

He moved away towards some chairs and they sat down. Deena wasn't a bit calm, she was terrified. Her heart was thudding and her synapses were exploding like fireworks.

"Couldn't you just ask questions instead of actually opening up my head to look in? I have a controller you know."

"I never thought of doing that. Who is your controller?"

"My ID."

"What form does this control take?"

"It governs my instincts and makes me what I am."

"And what are you?"

"I'm an obedient person and mostly adhere to the rules of my country. I try to be useful and helpful, good as opposed to bad."

"What a novel idea. Are all humans like this?"

"I'm afraid not."

"Why not?"

"Sometimes their workings become damaged or some parts are missing and that changes their behaviour. They oppose the rules and cause trouble."

"Does the ID punish them?"

"No. By then they are out of his control."

"Then who is in charge of them?"

"The devil."

He gestured to Deena's flask.

"What is that you are carrying? Is it a weapon?"

"No, it's coffee, my fuel."

"Can I taste it?"

Deena gave him some and he promptly spat it out.

"Is there a choice of fuel?"

"Yes. There is tea, water, hot chocolate and alcohol. You have to be wary of using alcohol though as it makes you overly familiar with complete strangers which can lead to stupid or dangerous behaviour."

He thought about all this for a while then asked,

"Do you want to go back to where I found you?"

"Very much."

"If I take you there could I talk to you again? All you have told me has been enlightening."

"Of course," Deena agreed somewhat shakily.

Next thing she knew she was alone, back in the wetlands still clutching her flask. She raced to her car, jumped in and locked the door. 'Quick, quick, get out of here,' she kept muttering aloud, over and over. When she got home she was astonished to see that she had only been gone for three hours. She went to a mirror and looked at her reflection. She hadn't altered at all. Did she dream the encounter this morning or had it really happened. She knew she would never go near these wetlands again. Just as she turned away from the mirror she noticed a sticker on the front of her jacket. The sort you get on a charity flag day when you pop some money in a collection box. Leaning closer she saw one word written on it.

Reprieved!

Where on Earth Have You Been?

by Moira McGee

My husband James has been gone for five days. I reported him missing after two. The police at my local station didn't appear too interested.

'Let's have your address then and someone will be along to get some details from you.'

'When?'

'Probably tomorrow, but let us know if he turns up before then.'

I went home but couldn't concentrate on doing anything. Just wandered from room to room. Out to the garden, in again. I wasn't so much worried as cross. How dare he bog off without a word and no phone calls? Thoughtless so-and-so. A Detective Constable and a lady Police Constable called the next day. I made coffee and, that done, we all sat down. The D.C. began the proceedings and the P.C. got out her notebook and pen.

'Could I have your husband's full name and occupation? He hasn't been home for three days now, right?'

I nodded.

'Has he done this sort of thing before?'

'No.'

Had an argument beforehand? Did you see him leave?'

'No and no.'

'Are any of his possessions missing? Clothes, money, passport?'

'Not that I can see.'

'How is your marriage, exactly? Happy?'

He must have sensed my slight hesitation because he sat up straighter in his chair and began to look more interested.

'We've been married a long time and don't live in each other's pocket,' I said defensively.

'Any children?'

'No.'

'Do you suspect him of being unfaithful?'

'I've never really given the idea much thought.'

'You don't seem too bothered by the idea though. Maybe you've been unfaithful and he's had enough.'

'This story you've just dreamed up is of little help in finding him,' I said with a sigh.

'Do you want him found?'

'Of course I do. Why do you think I came to you lot to report it?'

Was I being labelled a liar, I wondered. Maybe they'd start digging up the garden. That, at least, would be positive and a great help to me.

'More coffee?' I offered. Both of them were regarding me speculatively.

'No thanks, that's all for now, we'll be in touch. Do you have a recent photo of your husband we could have?'

I gave them a photo. I was relieved to see them leave and wondered why I was beginning to feel guilty. Another week passed with no word from either James or the police. As my husband freelanced with oil companies all around the globe I had no-one I could call for any information about his whereabouts. We were often separated for long spells and I was quite used to it but always knew where he was and he usually called me frequently.

Then the police did phone to say they would arrive shortly with a search warrant. I asked what they were going to search for to be told they'd know when they found it. Later several men arrived, some in white overalls with equipment plus a couple of uniforms with shovels. When I opened my mouth to speak one of them waved a piece of paper at me and told me to step aside and sit down somewhere out of the way. I went into the kitchen and leant on the edge of the sink, looking out of the window and thinking that this will be the most fun my neighbours have had in years.

'What the hell is going on?' There stood James holding his battered carry-on bag.

'Where on earth have you been?' I yelled. 'They were beginning to believe I'd done away with you.'

This said, I burst into tears. He dropped the bag and took me in his arms.

'What is it, what's happened? Between sobs I tried to explain.

'But I left you a note because you were out and it was an emergency as usual.'

'I didn't find any note.'

'C'mon, I'll show you where I left it.'

We went into the bedroom, fortunately still un-searched and James foraged around. He finally pulled out the blanket chest at the end of the bed and there it was, on the floor, a small white envelope.

'I'm so sorry darling, I never dreamt you wouldn't find it and the area I was in was hopeless for phone connections. Now, hadn't we better call off this search and apologise to everyone?'

Later, in the kitchen, holding mugs of hot tea liberally laced with duty free whisky, James took my hand, smiled and said,

'It's time we had a long talk. Enough of this non-communication, don't you agree?'

Gravity

by Moira McGee

Planet Prattle is east of the sun and west of the moon, smallish, with a population around 1 million. I won't bore you with the physical description of the inhabitants, suffice it to say, that to an Earthling, they are not easy on the eye. Their planet is dependent on a large red ball they've named Gravity and they have a special squadron of males on shift guarding it around the clock. They are a mostly happy race as their name might suggest and are quite unaware that they are being spied on.

Planet Pallid is their nearest neighbour and the ones with the covetous eyes. In every area of life there are bullies and others seeking new areas to conquer. With the Pallidsiders it wasn't that angle as much as their necessity for some new blood. They were fed up with each other's gloomy exteriors and weary ways. They needed a pep-up, some joy in their lives. From their observations of the Prattleaidians they held the key. A bit of inter-breeding between the two could be the answer, the trick being how to achieve this co-operation.

Now you and I might have suggested an exchange of e-mails or a visit from a delegation bearing gifts and inducements but that was not their way. They much preferred a bit of cloak and dagger, figuratively speaking, not war or bloodshed. A lot of talk ensued amongst the leaders so finally, Eureka! Steal Gravity. That way Prattle would be dragged out of its orbit, hurtle across to Pallid and stick on to it. The leaders went into another huddle the outcome of which was 'The great idea.' Firstly request a friendly visit and when there show an interest in seeing the Gravity ball. Do a reconnaissance of the area, surreptitiously, and report back. Then, on the first moonless night, send an inter-planetary vehicle containing a dozen or so stealthy, quick-thinking males who would be carrying Pallid Paralysers. Similar to stun guns but much more cool.

The visit was enjoyable and made the Pallidsiders want even more to mix in with the Prattleaidians. However, their mistake was, underestimation. The Prattleaidians were chatty, friendly and open but stupid they were not. They noticed the scarcely concealed interest of the delegates and the hot greedy look in their eyes when they viewed Gravity. Something was definitely afoot from pedestrian Planet Pallid. The Prattleaidians were more than ready for them when the raid eventually took place and retaliation was swift and sure. It culminated in the outwitted Pallid crew being rolled back into their vehicle, willy-nilly, sprawling everywhere and aimed back to their own planet.

After this debacle the Pallidsiders had to resort to Plan B. Earth was the next nearest planet. Their reasoning was that Earth contained so many people anyway that half a million, here or there, wouldn't be missed. Many light years later, during one gloomy evening, a fleet of space ships descended and scattered across Earth. The required number of Earthlings were quickly gathered up and whisked away. So, who knows how many half relatives we may now have on Planet Pallid or here for that matter? Could be we've already met one or two.

Frances Schultz
In Memoriam

Frances used her writing to clarify her own life experiences, and therefore left a legacy for her children and grand-children. She was been a member of Tea Tree Gully Library Writers Group for over six years and said the structured topics each month provided the discipline she needed to organise her thoughts and values.

Hats and Memories

by Frances Schultz

She was sitting comfortably in her easy chair, warmly nestled between the layers of her crocheted, black fringed, kaleidoscope medallions crafted by her ever busy fingers. The sun's rays added warmth and illuminated the brightly coloured flowers in the garden. Her world had shrunk to this one room which housed the bare necessities for living. Everything else had gone. Either been sold or given away along with her independence.

Where had the time gone? It had seemed no time at all since overcoming the shyness of childhood, the raising of children and sharing twilight years with her husband. They had been good years. Now she was alone with no-one to share her memories.

She stretched to retrieve the maroon gold embossed photo album, fingering its basket-weave texture before flicking through the well-worn black pages with their sepia photos slotted into place. She could still picture the colours that had been there. Was life more black and white in those innocent days? Was everything either right or wrong then? Nowadays, with maturity and a deeper understanding of issues, there seems to be more shades of grey.

Life had taken its twists and turns and she always wondered why. One of her Cockney father's favourite sayings was,

'They're like that because of the way their mother put their hat on.'

Hats...there weren't many hats in her album. In fact there was a distinct shortage of hats. There she was wearing a wide-brimmed straw garden hat whilst straddling a tiny tricycle. She could never understand why such a big child should be sitting on a miniature trike. Perhaps it was wartime austerity.

The next hat was only a hat in name. It was a pink frothy muslin concoction that adorned her hair when she was bridesmaid at her uncle and new aunt's wedding. She also remembered the soft texture of this first full length dress and the confetti snowflakes that swirled and rested on her rosebud posy. She savoured this moment in the spotlight. It was many years before she was a bridesmaid again.

She spied herself wearing a hand-knitted dark brown 'Brownie' beanie knitted by Aunt Daisy. Aunt Daisy was her Brown Owl's aunt who became an important part of her life for many years. Closing her cloudy, cataract eyes she could still remember the smell of the crispy, salt-encrusted sentry fingers of bacon that guarded the slightly undercooked poached eggs, cooked by Aunt Daisy on 'Pack Holidays' at Welwyn Garden City.

Her mind jumped from this image to the memory of children chasing a beanie-topped child in the school playground, knocking off the hat to reveal a shaven head and laughing unkindly. In those days anyone with head lice was treated in this cruel manner.

Another photo showed a stony beach dotted with boldly striped deck chairs. There she was with a red, shirred bathing costume clinging to her pubescent figure accentuating her white parchment skin. Long hair covered by a flying-helmet style, rubber bathing hat, snugly held in place by a silver buckled strap. No wonder her parents had migrated to Australia, land of golden beaches.

Holiday camp photos depicted the next two hats. One was a red, white and blue crepe pill-box paper hat worn to commemorate the Queen's Coronation. This was a part of the weekly scheduled entertainment for the 'happy campers' from London. The other hat was like a living tubular advertisement which bemoaned the cancellation of the Whist Drive. It topped off a mini, green crepe dress covered with playing cards. She shivered. All those people, all those 'happy campers' and the organised entertainment. Her tastes had changed over the years when she preferred travelling around Australia with her husband, exploring the country and experiencing its solitude.

Now she was growing tired with the heaviness of memories. The final hat was a lavender coloured circle of satin flowers attached to a headband with soft lace netting shielding her eyes. A bridesmaid again! Those vivid blue eyes looked back at her full of freshness and wonder at the beginning of adulthood and an unknown future.

No more time, no more hats, but a treasure trove of memories.

Mildred Bourn

Hello! My name is Mildred Bourn. I gave up hope of ever being a real writer when I finally accepted that I would never be able to come close to James Joyce. I do have one trait that I share with him. I spend hours with pen poised desperately searching in my head for the right word or phrase that will exactly convey my meaning. The difference being, he gets it right. Even though the great novel is beyond me I like to write. I belong to the writing group where the real reward is that I get the opportunity to listen to the work of my friends and to share ideas and skills. The art of composition has importance for me because it makes me clear my mind of the mundane and move onto a higher plane.

Too Many Old Books

by Mildred Bourn

Solution! Read all the tatty old paperbacks and then dispose of them.

Made a good start! Picked up the tattiest and least remembered children's literature book crowded with all the others of the same ilk on the shelf.

Well would you believe it? The first chapter definitely rang a bell. Buying groceries from a train, known as "The Tea and Sugar."

Yep! You've guessed it in one. "The Min-Min" which was written by Mavis Thorpe Clark! Well I figured it would do for a start!

Do for a start?

I was captivated. I was enraptured. I read on and on through the yellowing pages that kept falling out of the book. The story is improbable, two dimensional and impossible to believe. Everybody should read it. {I won't lend you my copy.}

1966 was a good year. It was the year our small family arrived in Australia. It was the year our Australian baby was born. It was the year that Mavis Thorpe Clark published The Min-Min. This book is a slab of contemporary history of its time.

Points of interest are the absence of the mother throughout. She was faceless in the bedroom, not well, being taken cups of tea. In contrast is the lady living in the outback sheep station. No-one could be really that nice. Did they really cook over wood fired stoves and bake in wood fired ovens in the house kitchen when the temperature was plus 40 degrees outside?

The book is as much about fatherhood as anything else. There he was living at a railway siding with his five kids and an ailing wife, working on the rail tracks all day, loving his family but not taking proper care of them. It was no wonder. Then being berated by the magistrate for his ineptitude in letting his son run amok.

A happy ending is had by all. Here comes the bit that makes this book a national treasure. They live happily ever after in a housing trust home in Whyalla where the future is assured for all of them.

Oh, Ms. Thorpe Clark, the sheer happiness in ignorance of what was to come. The lady wrote a book, in good faith, in her comfortable home in Melbourne.

Out of the Mist

by Mildred Bourn

It had all been so good then. Grandma had taken him to the hospital to see mummy. She had bought him some sweets on the way. That was a treat on its own as he was not usually allowed to have nearly as many sweets as he wanted. When they got up to the ward, Mummy had a special present all wrapped up in fancy paper for him. When he opened it he was so pleased, it was a racing car to match his set of toy cars at home.

Only after all that did they wheel in a bassinet with a little red wrinkly baby in it. By this time Daddy had arrived and they all cooed and smiled at the baby. He was lifted up to give it a light kiss on the forehead. He didn't want to leave without Mummy but he was assured they would come back next day and they would all go home together. The promise was kept and when they got there she was all dressed and ready to leave. She picked up the baby blanket with the baby in it and started to walk to the door.

"We are not taking it home with us are we?

"Yes, Tom, of course we are. He is your little baby brother, James, and we will look after him."

"Can't they look after him here?

"No!" said Daddy, "We are going to look after him, and keep him safe and love him. We are all going to protect him.

As it eventuated, it was mainly him who had to protect the little perisher. All through school he was dragged in to break up fights that might get him hurt, get him down from high branches of trees and drive would-be bullies away. There were countless times when he was playing with his mates and someone would come and get him to sort out a problem. It was not that the kid was fragile or anything of that sort. Just the opposite in fact, the parents would often tell people what a dare devil their younger son was. No mention of who had to look out for him and keep getting him out of trouble all the time. So it went on right up to adulthood.

"What about the trouble with the girl?"

He stopped the reminiscing right there.

He could hear the voices behind him as he stood on the windswept floodplain alone. No one approached him. No one else had been allowed to go that far. By the same token no one had been prepared to stop him. It had been a few years since he went away, he knew them all and they knew him. They had been a local family. He had been told that the team of workmen who had gone up to the water mains had been able to stop the flood and now they were all safe. The team had been sent back down by the boss and only he had stayed to make sure all the safeguards held.

Their jubilation had turned to worry now because the boss had not come down yet and it had been many hours. The authorities had vetoed any suggestion that a search party go back up with the reasonable argument that it would be putting too many lives at risk. Dusk was falling and the danger grew for the lone man up the hill. The other lone man stood and listened to the voices behind him.

The shrill voice of a little girl was saying, "Mummy why is he staying there all alone?"

"Because he has to stay there, Darling," she answered.

"But who is making him stay...?"

The voices faded away. He knew exactly why he had to stay. He was waiting for interest to wane so that he could set off up the hill to search. Then suddenly he started to run squelching through the mud to where he had seen the faint light bobbing up and down.

Twenty minutes later the crowd watched as he staggered out of the falling darkness half carrying, half dragging an almost inert figure.

"Mummy, he just slapped his face really hard and now he is hugging him. Why is he doing that?

"He is probably trying to stop him losing consciousness and then trying to keep him warm."

He was getting closer and he heard the child calling. He could only concentrate on the task in hand, they were getting close to the ambulance crew, and he called out to them for help. Only then did they come with a stretcher to carry the barely conscious man. Still the two men clung to each other.

EPILOGUE

The woman with her child watched as the two men she had loved so much were driven away in the ambulance. She remembered how people said it was girl trouble that drove the older brother away. It wasn't quite like that. It was true that she had set her heart on James, and when he tried to drop her she had made a fuss. As always Tom had stepped in and sorted everything out. She became Tom's girlfriend instead. This relationship had not been the light kissy sort she had had with James. She went up north to her parent's home to have her baby. When Tom arrived, they had married shortly before their little girl was born. They had not returned to live here, this was a visit.

The child had been fretful and she had taken her into bed with her. Later he returned, went to his daughter and kissed her gently. He walked round the bed and got in next to her. "Sorry love, I had to sort him out."

She sighed.

Poppy

by Mildred Bourn

POPPY
I wish I'd never met that cat.
Now I've said it, and that is that.
She only ever comes to stay
When her other servants are away.
Her personal chef sent her victuals
with instructions on eating rituals.
We were the owners of this house
Or so we thought! Me and my spouse!
Then came the day the cat moved in.
We were subdued. Never to win!
She sometimes comes when we call: "Poppy!"
But not always, so don't get soppy.
She arrived on the appointed day
Checked around to see if she'd stay!
She did not greet us with a catlike smile.
Just checked to see if 'twas worthwhile.
I forgot to say she is good looking
But strictly forbids picking upping.
We the staff must know our place
No familiarity towards her grace.
Oh yes I wish I'd never met her
I thought mature people would know better.
But I've fallen for her now you see
And devoted I will forever be.
Reciprocation is a lost hope
My broken heart will just have to cope
She shares our nuptial couch at night
And acts as though this is her right.
Now I don't know where I'm at,
I wish I'd never met that cat.

I am a Bus Stop

by Mildred Bourn

I am a bus stop. I used to think I was a ghost, but now I know I am a bus stop. I stand there on the side of the road. People come and stand right next to me and behave exactly as if I wasn't there. They talk to each other totally excluding me.

Some bus stops are tall and slim. They stand alone all dressed in yellow or even red on the busy roads. I don't envy them. Folk just lean on them or, if they are juveniles, they grab them with one hand and use them to swing around. I am more of a disembodied head fixed to a Stobie pole which carries cables overhead and also has a street light sticking out over the road. Once in place I am pretty well maintenance free. There are some bus stops that have the luxury of shelters with seats adjacent to them. Fat lot of good it does them. They are left outside to fend for themselves.

I am not totally isolated, you know. I have a neighbour. We don't have much in common. My neighbour is red and tends to be obese with a wide mouth. People come along and feed my neighbour with what looks like slices of stale white bread. I watch in disdain. I am not jealous, so you needn't think it. You see I know what comes later:- this red van draws up next to us. What follows is almost too horrible to relate. My neighbour is literally disembowelled and the white slices taken away

I know well that I belong to a dying breed. I see it all from my vantage point. I watch the bright, late-model tin-mobiles race past me. They are totally oblivious of my existence. They have no use for me now. I belong to the past. Even so I still have power. The largest of the mobile metal vehicles comes to a stop before me. I have become aware that it takes an individual with movable parts to make that happen. No longer does my presence force the halt. It also needs a raised hand. However this is dependent on a symbiotic relationship. They could raise a hand all they like but it only works when standing next to me.

So now you know I am a bus stop. Oh, you well may raise an argument against this posit, saying that a bus stop is stationary and I am not. Well, rest assured, it is only a matter of time because my immobility is increasing at a rate of knots. Don't be concerned about the contradiction of grammatical logic in that last sentence. I am unbustoppable. Look that up in your Funk and Wagnall's.

Villains

by Mildred Bourn

I am called a villain and that is not fair, nor is it true. I am the victim of the worst form of racial abuse which is indefensible since the perpetrators are on a totally different modus of communication than my kind have. I have many admirable qualities. I am strong, resourceful, have good teeth, am quick thinking and I have a friendly approach. I was born to live a hard life, living on the same planet but a different plane than my verbal assailants. I spend my life in an inhospitable dark forest. It is freezing cold at night. In order to survive in these conditions I absolutely must have a rich protein diet. The odd rabbit or mouse or rat is simply not enough.

That Red riding Hood story is a typical example of the bad press I get all the time. The whole piece is pure fiction of course. The so-called potential victim doesn't even have a name of her own. She is only known by the outfit she wears. What a "goodie-goodie" she is, and what an uncaring mother she is blighted with. I ask you, who in their right mind would send a young girl to walk through the woods alone to her Nanna's house? So she is sending a basket of food for her sick mother. Balderdash!

The story goes that I accosted her and extracted information about the grandmother, where she lived, and also her weak state of health. What comes next is ridiculous. The gullible reader is expected to believe that this wolf, so evil, will spare the nice young meaty meal to hot-foot it to the old crone's house in order to damage his teeth on the skin, bone and gristle to be had there. That is an insult to my intelligence.

On the subject of intelligence, these fanciful storytellers fail to acknowledge that the so-called man's best friend that so many of their kind fuss over is in fact a direct descendant of my pure breed. Why do you suppose even vegetarians feed meat to their dog? Oh and the outcry when the sweet little poodle nips someone. For all the clever breeding purity will out. I live a life of fear because humans are always trying to kill me. They don't hunt me for food they just kill because they don't like me. Well I don't like them with their firesticks that kill from a distance in a disassociated manner.

I am respectful to my food source. They are free to live a carefree life right up to the moment of demise. So what do humans do with their cows, pigs and sheep? Answer me that! They drag them off somewhere out of the way don't they? I present myself personally to my prospective meal and kill in proximity. Last but not least, I do not leave my prey to rot. I always eat the lot.

Joanne Baker

Joanne Baker is a prize winning poet who has been published in several magazines and anthologies. In May 2013 she published her first anthology: The Journey to Here, Ginninderra Press.

Since her book launch Joanne has been a recipient of a Richard Llewellyn Emerging Artist grant, been involved in the organisation and performed in, the 2013 Tea Tree Gully Poetry Festival, performed for the Langhorne Creek Writers Festival October 13th 2013 and ran a workshop and performed for the Strathalbyn Arts Feast on Australia day 2014. She has produced her own chapbook, A Very Strange Person, January 2014.

She has been guest speaker and regular reader at Gawler poets at the pub and was the Treasurer of North Eastern Writers incorporated (NEWinc.) for three years. North Eastern Writers have hosted an open mic night as part of the Adelaide Fringe, Joanne has been the MC for the last two years. During February 2014 and 2015 Joanne performed for the Salisbury Secret Garden as part of the Adelaide Fringe.

Her Poem 'Bushfire in the Gully' was a feature of the Tea Tree Gully Trail of Tails in 2016. Joanne was interviewed on local radio station PBA-FM (89.7FM) on the 4th March 2014. Since November 2014 she has been a regular panellist on PBA-FM's show Words Out Loud. On the 24th February 2015 she debuted as a host of Words Out Loud. She is an active co-host of PBA-FM's Wednesday weekly chat show, The Kitchen Table, as well as host of an hour-long music show 9am every Tuesday.

Joanne combines rich details, sharp observations and a wild imagination with rhythm and rhyme in her memorable poems.

Cutting the Stone
by Joanne Baker

The box was locked, the key stashed away
guilty were silent, there was nothing to say
sentence was passed, no tears ever shed
perpetual punishment, better off dead.

Impossible burden, yet still it was borne
Sandpaper buffing, sharp edges get worn
Strength under pressure, sometimes too tough
Far harder than stone, a diamond in rough.

The more she was burnished, the clearer her gaze
Scoured away all superfluous haze
Bad habits broken, doors welded shut
From the box she exploded
And the Diamond was cut.

A Minority of One
by Joanne Baker

I want to dazzle you with poetry
To haunt you with my rhyme
Seduce you with some similes
And alliterate at times.

I'd drag you to my darkest tale
Dress your wounds if there was need
I'd sharpen up your trusty sword
And I'd watch you then succeed.

Every poem would be an adventure
And I'd be by your side
A friendship beyond measure
True love has never lied.

And there my shaking hand would stop
For the truth is plain to me
I stay the pathetic practitioner
Of love-lorn poetry.

Roshana Ferrie

Roshana has been with the group for over seven years now and loves the fun interaction with her fellow group members and all she learns from monthly workshops. The challenge of writing to the set topics can sometimes be just that – a challenge. However they are not set in concrete and we can opt to read a chapter from an ongoing piece if we so choose.

Fashion *Faux Pas*

by Roshana Ferrie

The salty flood poured forth, drenching everything in its path as it made its self-pitying way down her cheeks, trickling uncomfortably into her hair as she lay on her back on her bed. How embarrassing! She'd never felt so ashamed in her life. She could feel her face turn scarlet and burn, burn, burn, all over again. Thank goodness she hadn't known anybody there or she'd never be able to leave home again... No! Wait! This wasn't a pity party – she was mad, pissed off, and feeling righteous about her anger. He was the ignorant, selfish, thoughtless male who'd placed her in that embarrassing position. He'd asked her to the dance. A casual dance, at the Manly Town Hall, he said. They hold them quite frequently, said he. Oh yes!

This was to be their first date, and mum had worked hard and made her a lovely shift dress in soft wool; yellow with a black design and a cream coloured skivvy – also new. Her black boots would finish the outfit off nicely. It was a sharp, modern outfit, perfect for a casual dance at the Manly Town Hall in 1965.

When he'd come to pick her up he was neatly and casually attired in pants and a short sleeved shirt so she'd felt completely comfortable with what she was wearing. Pretty even. He was polite to her parents and chatted away to them before they headed off.

On the way he announced he just had to pop into a friend's place for a moment to get changed. 'Changed?' asked she. 'Nothing to worry about' said he. Stupid man. When he re-appeared he's now wearing a tuxedo, a very nice tuxedo but somehow no longer matching comfortably with her casual dance attire.

She queried this change and repeated the words he'd used when he asked her out. 'You look great,' he said. 'Nothing to worry about.' She wanted to go home and change but he was adamant that she looked fine and home was now miles away. 'Too far,' said he. So on they went, with her stress levels rising every mile further they went from home.

It was just as she feared. The knots in her stomach and up her neck hurt even more as she gazed out the passenger side window. He parked the car, helped her out and up the stairs they went with all the tuxedoed "gents" and their glamorous ball gown clad dates. She was the only female not dressed for a ball, not a casual dance, but a fancy, formal ball.

He introduced her to the other members of their table, all appropriately dressed, naturally enough, with her as the ugly duckling. She felt completely humiliated and beat a hasty retreat to the very elegant powder room which of course only made her feel even worse. Two of the other women had followed her and soon had the story and were suitably furious with the ignoramus Harry for putting her in that unenviable position. Without their cheerful company and sympathy, she probably would have tried to hike home to Killara away across the other side of the city, or better yet, tried to steal both his car keys and the car they fitted.

But as she had been brought up knowing it was "naughty" to take other people's belongings, she refrained. She held her head up and went out and danced, rather well actually, no doubt thanks to all the dance courses she had taken with her best friend, Lynne. She tried, very hard, not to envision punching his lights out as she glided around the floor. Dropping him on his head, she could have managed quite ably, having nearly four years of judo under her belt, so to speak. Both those options however, she knew would have been more "naughties" so placed them in her mental "refrain from" list.

By the end of the evening even Harry had managed to work out that he'd made a rather large and horrendous blunder as his mates were now giving him a hard time and their dates were hen-pecking him supposedly in good fun but with sharp, cutting beaks.

The trip home wasn't quite as much fun as the stressful one to Manly and funnily enough, was a deathly quiet journey. Neither forgiven nor forgotten at this stage and I really had nothing I could say politely. Poor Harry, it turned out, didn't know the difference between a ball and a dance and certainly not a formal ball gown and a casual dance outfit. Poor Harry! Well he certainly knew after that date. The request for another date was vehemently but politely refused – to, no doubt, great relief on both sides as she leapt agilely from the car and beat a hasty retreat to her front door. No goodnight kiss for poor Harry.

The following weekend, her parents showed her an article in The Sydney Morning Herald. It seemed an early morning raid at young Harry's residence had uncovered a rather large cache of illegal arms and ammo. He had been under surveillance for some time and was currently under arrest and helping the police with their ongoing investigation.

After his trial ended it was go directly to jail. Poor Harry. And at Lindfield, one very smart tuxedo sat gathering dust in his wardrobe.

'Good escape,' said Dad.

Dawn Dreaming

by Roshana Ferrie

Strident Mynah birds announce their presence from clumps of palms beyond the sandy dunes Jen has just dispiritedly trudged over. Today she barely notices when dawn's pastel hues spread across sky and sea. They break the darkness, bringing colour and softness with them. Nor does she notice the small waves that shush in, hurrying over cool, wet sand to greet dryness, still warm from yesterday's summer heat. They splash over her feet and ankles where she now stands at the water's edge.

Dawn has become her favourite time of day; no-one to disrupt this tranquillity, this blessed silence when she can briefly be alone with only her thoughts for company. No camera-encrusted tourists have yet arrived, to gawk, with loud exclamations, at all the beauty she has always taken for granted; no other locals are walking with their unrestrained, yappy dogs.

It still feels wonderfully cool at this early hour, helped by the usual impudent sea-breeze that scampers its way ashore to ruffle her hair into untidy curls before tugging playfully at her old clothes. She doesn't laugh at it today as she used to, but remains staring listlessly out to sea as incoming waves splash further up her legs.

Jen walks higher up the beach and flops into what she regards as 'her' spot; her 'Thinking Spot', as she and mum had laughingly named it, with comfortable, deep, dry sand above high tide mark, and an ancient, time-smoothed log to provide a back rest. Closing her eyes, she breathes in the familiar salty smell of the sea that washes the shore only metres from her feet, and tries to relax in this brief moment of uninterrupted peace that has lately become a rare occurrence. Mum had always made sure she had alone time on the beach. Now there is not even school to provide an outlet.

Silence, with only birds... Ah! Raucous Mynahs are now in slightly more musical mode, joining all the other feathered singers in their daily dawn greeting. How many times has she listened, rapt, in this very spot, to that early morning chorus? Nowadays, she can recognise all the individual types of birds, all doing their own thing, yet somehow it manages to blend as harmoniously as her school choir. Jen realise how much she misses the singing and the company of all her friends.

Eyes still closed, she listens intently again... waves, still shush in... and the salt-laden breeze now wafts over her, as if sensing her mood, then gently rustles nearby leaves before it scurries impishly away, over the empty dunes, through the palms beyond with a flurry and rattle of empty seed pods. It sounds just like Joe when he, equally impishly, tries sneaking up on her peace and quiet and the rattly, empty seed pods give him away.

But for now, undisturbed by anything human, she slumps, lost in vivid daydreams as her mind meanders along a dozen paths, and her dreams roam unrestricted. Different careers and lives/lifestyles unfold in her colourful and artistic imagination. All the options she and her mum had either playfully or seriously considered swirl around in her head like the glowing patterns in Annie's toy kaleidoscope.

Well, she most definitely does not want to be an astronaut and bounce around, weightless, in a clumsy looking spacesuit, either on the moon, or in all that red dust on Mars. Besides, as she always feels sick on the school bus, no doubt she'd truly be sick in a space ship. Being a fireman, no, firewoman, or fireperson if she really wants to be politically correct, certainly isn't on her list either! These are Joe's daydreams, not hers. What's going on here?

How about singing in front of a few thousand screaming fans, as her own rock band blares away around her? Mum was always saying she had a beautiful voice, especially when she sang the twins to sleep. Even though she might enjoy the rock and roll part, she wouldn't want to be caught up in the sex and drugs that seem to be such a part of that scene. They definitely aren't on her agenda. Anyway, it's Annie that wants to be the famous rock star, not her.

Now she sees herself looking like a typical student, walking the paths of a campus, deep in fascinating and friendly conversation with other students. This is more like it! Jen notes the design portfolio tucked under one arm, and tries to read the titles of the books her dream self holds in her other hand. Are they for a TAFE or university course? Before she can decipher them, her imagination draws her irresistibly elsewhere.

She is clad in designer clothes, not this tatty outfit she is wearing, and is strutting down a catwalk, with other stunningly dressed models. Silks, satins, materials she can't even name, flow seductively or cling sinuously to slender forms. People, important-looking people are smiling at her, admiring the beautifully designed clothes she is displaying. Turning at the end of the runway, back straight and head proudly up, she parades down the walkway. Maybe one day she really will be one of those models, not just daydreaming about it. Or even better, stunning clothes like that will carry her tag in them and she will be the famous designer.

Whisking through the curtains at the end of the catwalk, her mind flows on from the richness of the clothes just seen. It flows to the lushness of the art masterpieces she and mum pored over in the books she regularly borrowed from the school library.

Jen feels her eyes begin to burn, then overflow, as bitter, bereft tears weave tracks down her face to drip onto her t-shirt. She remembers the two of them endlessly studying their favourites, the brilliant, coloured reproductions in those borrowed books. Done silently, secretly, at night, when everyone else was safely and deeply asleep. She and mum had so admired the skilled techniques used; quietly oohed and aahed over the sumptuousness of the colour and the intricate detail in the costumes and settings. The paintings were so life-like that they felt they could reach out and touch the softness of skin, run fingers through the gleam of ringlets, straight hair or soft, curly beards, even step in to join the adoring throng.

So often, she and her mum had laughed and giggled together, muffling their companionship in cupped hands, even the tea towel one night, so no one would overhear. Her mum had encouraged her, scrimping and saving from the housekeeping to buy needed paper, pencils and paints, so that one day, soon, Jen would go away to study those skills.

That had been their secret dream, shared by only the two of them. Jen would escape this drab existence, this humdrum life, and mum would finally experience it through her. That seemed only fair, as mum had been forced by her own ma and pa to give up her dreams.

Night after night, they'd stayed up, hunched companionably together over the old wooden table in the kitchen as Jen firstly finished homework or worked on assignments. Mum had been so proud of her, knowing that Jen would be the first in the family to ever finish High School, let alone go on to TAFE, or maybe even uni. She wasn't going to let anything, or anyone, stop that from happening this time. But only late at night was safe, when all other tedious yet necessary family chores were complete and Jen's school work was safely packed away for the morning. Then and only then had come the very best part of all – their cherished book sharing time. Valuable books, priceless time!

'Oi! Whatcha doin' Sis? Jeez, ya should 'ear Dad! He's madder 'n a hornet at ya. He said git ya backside home now or yer in big trouble. What a racket – the twins 'r' squawkin' for their bottle; Joe's havin' a wreckin' competition with Annie. Jus' wait'll ya see tha place, there's gonna be lotsa jobs for ya t'day, all 'cos you aint there to sort 'em out an' get us brekkie. Serves ya right! We got things ta be doin' too, us blokes. Yeah,

I jus' knewed you'd be wastin' time out 'ere as usual. Selfish cow... You's got responses... repondas... res... oh you know wot I mean! Ya gotta look afta the littlies now, so ain't no point sittin' out 'ere bawlin' like a baby. There's enuf o' them back 'ome already, so move ya arse, girl.'

Yellow Angels

by Roshana Ferrie

I didn't realise it at the time. I should have but I just didn't see it. Of course it was really obvious looking back on it. However, stuck in the middle of the mess, and distracted by everything going on around me, it was anything other than clear. Besides, I'd never owned a house before and had no idea that could happen.

The tropical rain had been pelting down for days. A more or less constant wash of water against the windows and doors that blew up under the tin on the roof until it found spots to sneak in and run onto the ceiling. The monotonous plink, plink, plink as it hit the bottom of every bucket, pot and pan in the place was driving me nuts. I had been putting a face washer in the bottom to absorb some of the noise but had run out of them very quickly and was loath to waste one of my soft, new towels by cutting it up. That meant I had to put up with the irritating noise and try to ignore the rain ruining the ceilings of my new house.

I stood at the window and watched the muddy, coffee-coloured waters of the flooded creek as it rushed, frothing and churning, between me and the relative safety of the road beyond. The little flat bridge that was the only exit from the property was already mostly underwater. It had been rickety and rattly for the month since I had moved in and was probably even more of a shambles now with dangerous gaps where the speed and pressure of the raging waters had effortlessly ripped out heavy planks and flung them down stream. Well I wouldn't be making a dash for safety by that route and my "To do" list was growing longer every minute.

The jitters were making the hair on the back of my neck stand on end. The water from the creek reached the top of the bank and began to slither, like a long brown snake, down the gentle slope towards me. There was nothing to stop it inundating the house. There were no sand bags blocking any of the doors. That had been top of the "To do" list but... Well no point in making excuses, it was too late now and they weren't going to help.

I paced up and down, checking out the front windows then going to check out the back. The rain still rained and the water still rose all around. I was pointlessly hoping that the house would rise up like Noah's ark and float above the damaging flood waters but had a feeling that was not going to happen. Back and forth I paced again, from one end of the house to the other, wearing a track in the already worn carpet.

The water lapped at the door then slid under it looking like that deadly brown snake again. I rushed to gather up sheets, towels, bedding, anything to stop the threatening flow, and stuffed them in front of both doors. I was cursing myself for not having done it earlier when the water was merely threatening and not actually making inroads into my lounge room. I cursed myself again for not buying that new battery when I'd begun to have trouble starting the car. Today, of course, the battery was dead as the proverbial dodo and my car sat in the carport – a lump of useless metal. I could, however, push it out of the carport a little, and use it as a ladder to climb onto the carport roof – if the water rose high enough to make that a necessity.

I sighed and stood in the middle of the lounge looking around at my ancient, scratched furniture and working out which was the highest to perch on before I had to take to the outside. I chose my buffet. It wasn't made of solid timber so I hoped it wouldn't fall to pieces when surrounded by water. I grabbed the foldout kitchen footstool and put it in front of it then turned and picked up a couple of the big lounge cushions to use as padding. I may as well be as comfortable as I could possibly be if I was going to be perched on a buffet for hours.

They actually saved my life, believe it or not, because as I about-faced, there was a horrid cracking roar. I shrieked as the weighty ceiling gave way, and fell on me, flinging me to the carpet. It inundated me with forty years of dirt, now mud, old insulation and yucky water that had been sitting in the roof and hadn't escaped through the leak holes. The water rushed in all directions, flooding the lounge and washing the home made "door stop" away. A new stream poured in under the now unblocked doorway to join what was already there.

The SES team that came in a boat checking everyone up and down the creek saw my car in the carport and looked through the window. They saw the flooded lounge room and a foot sticking out from under the ceiling that was now the floor. The door was jammed so they broke a window guessing that time could be vital.

They were right. The weight crushing me was pushing my face further into the gap between the cushions. Water lapped at my mouth and I struggled to draw a breath into my nose but the heaviness pushing me down was making it too hard, I was gasping through my nose and everything around me was fading to grey, then black.

I dreamed I could hear voices, far, far away but my brain refused to compute the words into an understandable language. Sounded more like double Dutch or Greek to me. Then I dreamed I could breathe again and that hands were lifting me and carrying me and rocking me and all the time I coughed and coughed and coughed. I opened my eyes and the rain flooded them. I swear it wasn't tears, it was rain and I was being rocked in a boat rowed by people in yellow jackets and pants with SES printed on them.

Yellow angels, that's what they were and would always be, to me.

Death by Chocolate

by Roshana Ferrie

Decree Nisi. Only one more month and it's all over and done with. The cheating bastard! Hope his little silicon-boobed fluff bunny is enjoying his burps, farts and window-rattling snores more than I ever did. They deserve each other. I don't know whether to laugh or cry. No. I am never going to cry over them again. But I do want chocolate. I've lost 15 kilos. I want chocolate. I deserve chocolate.

I'm going to have a hot chocolate, a great big one and a piece of chocolate mud cake and I'm going to have it in the new bakery around the corner.

I pulled out my phone and arranged with my sister Phoebe to meet her there.

She's brought her friend Susie.

'I feel sick,' I moan to them an hour later.

They look at each other and raise their eyebrows. 'Gee, I wonder why that might be?' said Phoebe in a sing-song voice.

'Can't imagine.' Susie laughed and rolled her eyes melodramatically.

'Don't be mean. Can't you see I'm suffering?'

'Self-induced mud cake suffering and over-indulgent behaviour – no sympathy! Time to stop wallowing in the past and get on with the rest of your life. Congrats on the weight loss, Kate, you look great.' Phoebe turned to Susie. 'I reckon she needs a makeover to top it all off, don't you Susie?'

'Oh no,' I whined. 'I'll be good. I'll get up early and go for a walk. I'll cut my chocolate intake down again.'

'Let's try the Plaza,' Susie said, totally ignoring me.

I sit rebelliously in front of the mirror, scowling so ferociously I'd frighten even a grizzly bear with toothache. How can I sulk if I'm looking good? I want to sulk. I'm feeling very sorry for myself. I should have stayed home and eaten chocolate by myself. No sympathy from Phoebe or Susie.

What are friends for? Look at them sitting over there grinning like the Cheshire cat – a pair of them. I could use them for matching bookends. And there are men in here too. I saw them when we came in. I don't want anything to do with men at the moment. Anyway they are probably all gay. Aren't all male hairdressers gay? No, of course they aren't. That sounds really homophobic, my girl. But that doesn't matter, they are still male with that *X* or is it *Y* chromosome? I can never remember which way it goes. Sheesh, I'm nervous. I'm rambling again.

'Surely it can't be that bad? Most people love to be pampered. A facial, haircut and colour sounds like a real pick-me-up.' I jump as a deep, melodious voice speaks from over my shoulder. I refuse to look in the mirror at the owner of it. Instead I grump, which suits my mood better.

'I hate facials. I really, really hate facials. All that goo clogging up my pores makes me feel as though I'm suffocating. And I've never, ever coloured my hair.'

'I can see that. It's beautiful and there are so many different tones threaded through it.' I felt him lift my long hair and let it flow over his hands. I still didn't look in the mirror. 'Well your hair is a bit dry and has a few split ends but it certainly doesn't need a colour. I would suggest a shampoo and a relaxing head massage then a deep moisturising treatment on it after a little trim. Should bring it up a treat and the facial is up to you. You might like a face massage and some moisturiser instead. If you feel like it of course, it's completely up to you.

A choice! I'm being offered a choice. I haven't been offered a choice by a male for a long time. A very, long time. What a pleasant change. I stop scowling and listen to the voice, goose bumps run down my arms and my head tingles where he is touching my hair. Colin Firth? Sean Connery? Could be either one of them. Whoever he sounds like, it's certainly making my hormones wake up from their lengthy nap.

I don't want to peep in case I am disappointed. Bet he's gay, or married, or too young. I refuse to be a cradle snatcher like that shitty soon to be ex-husband of mine. Oops, Mr Gorgeous Voice has finished talking.

I finally raise my head, then my eyes and look coolly in the mirror. Our eyes lock and my stomach leaps up into my throat then falls back into place.

'That sounds interesting – but no facial,' I manage to gulp out. I bet everyone just falls at his feet, well not me. I'm not falling for the smiling hazel eyes and shiny chestnut hair. Of course it's shiny, he's a hairdresser. Well he's just the right age, no wedding ring, but is he gay? He doesn't seem to be gay. There's no sign emblazoned on his forehead saying I am/am not gay. Sheesh he's cute. No. Not cute. Distinguished, with that dash of silver hair at his temples. Grab a hold of your imagination girl, before it floats out the door past the Cheshire cats.

A shampoo, moisturising treatment, hair trim and face massage later, I feel like a new woman and Mr Distinguished has done the lot. Surely that's unusual, especially as I find out that he owns the salon and has only popped in to see how his staff are doing. We have chatted companionably about all sorts of things, including Cheshire cats both real and literary, as he worked busily on my now pampered head. It feels so good I'm not about to argue with what he has done. He has fantastic, magical hands that match the voice and my imagination is running wild. Along with the goose bumps leaping up and down all over my body, my hormones are saying "ooh yes please. More! More!'

The Voice spoke. 'Hey, Ms Kate Dargie, you look even more gorgeous than when you came in, even if I do say so myself. How would you like to escape out the back door and have some lunch with me? You can pick up the Cheshire cats later.'

I couldn't help but burst out laughing and I laugh and laugh. It feels so good as I haven't done that for what seems like way too long.

'Yes please, I'd love to. As long as I can have a big, strong, hot chocolate.'

Rick Coy

Whilst Rick's main contribution to our group seems to be his work as our Secretary, he enjoys the meetings and the challenge of the topics we set each month. His 2012 book *Make 'em Laugh, Make 'em Laugh* wasn't a best seller but he has high hopes for his latest production, *Yoo Sed Wot?,* a short introduction to a study of the English language.

Rick has been the driving force behind the Glimpses trilogy and has edited each volume. Recently he has had articles published in the magazines 'ONECOTA', 'The Ensign', and '*e*Volve'.

The Back Story

by Rick Coy

I'm pretty sure it was early in 1961, on a Monday, when they first came. Though why my husband was home to answer the door, I can't remember. Maybe he was on a 'Rostered Day Off', or taking a 'sickie' or maybe the Railways just gave him a day to move into our new home. It doesn't matter really, he was home and answered the door to the three men. Two were in plain clothes with trilby hats on and had a special warrant and the third was in the khaki uniform of a Commonwealth Police Officer. I was in the kitchen, taking pots out of the cardboard boxes and putting them on the shelves and in the cupboards. I could hear the voices but I couldn't make out what they were saying. I was curious. I went down the passage to the front door.

Damian was speaking, "There must be a mistake. First my surname isn't 'Hamilton' and second we only moved into this house over the weekend."

"What's this all about?" I asked. The question was addressed to no-one in particular; anyone who knew the answer I guess.

"These gentlemen have a warrant for the arrest of a Duncan Hamilton; have you any idea who that can be?"

"No! The Colonel's name was Duncan, but his surname was Harrison not Hamilton. In fact, I don't know any Hamiltons at all."

"The Colonel?" queried the taller of the two plain clothes officers.

"Yes! He got us this house. He was the Real Estate agent for this area. He lived here, in this house when we lived in a Railway house at Hillcrest. We made enquiries up here at Tea Tree Gully and the Colonel said if we could wait a couple of weeks we could have this house as he and his wife were moving to Queensland. We just called him 'The Colonel' because he looked like one. You know, military bearing, small mustache, very proper. It was just our nickname for him. We never let him or his wife know we called him that."

"May we come in whilst we pursue our enquiries?" asked the officer.

"Of course. I'll make a cup of tea. Come into the kitchen."

When they were all seated around our kitchen table, the tall officer produced a sort of passport photograph. "Is this him," he asked.

Both Damian and I squinted at the photo. It was a youngish man in a khaki uniform.

"I think so," I said.

Damian said, "This was taken some time ago but it does look like a younger version of the Colonel. What's he done?"

The officer didn't answer that question but asked, "Did they leave a forwarding address?"

"No!" I said. "And that surprised me because Mrs Harrison and I got on really well. In the short time we knew them she and I became quite good friends. She was really, really nice; like someone's Nanna. The Colonel was nice too but he was more reserved; a little stand-offish. I would have liked to have their new address so that we could keep in touch."

"Tell me your story," said the officer to Damian.

"Well, we are 'ten pound poms' as you probably guessed. I studied Railway Engineering at Crewe where we lived. I did my 'City and Guilds' first and then a basic degree at Crewe Polytechnic. We applied at Australia House to come to Australia a couple of years ago, that was in 1957 wasn't it Love?" I nodded. "I was snapped up by the South Australian Railways. I work at the Islington Workshops, mainly on design and construction projects. And because the Railways and Mr Playford paid our fare, we got our ten pounds back from the Commonwealth. They gave us a temporary house at Hillcrest until we could sort ourselves out and buy our own place. The Colonel was very helpful to us and we got this place at the right price and the Colonel arranged things so we don't even have a second mortgage."

"Mmm!" said the officer. "Very commendable. But I'd like to say a couple of things to you, because if they do contact you, I want to know straight away. First, you are doing him a disservice by calling him 'The Colonel'. In fact he was a Major-General. In the Rhodesian Army actually, in charge of internal security. His job was to round up the blacks who were harassing the white farmers. He and his men were not very fussy when it came to human rights, torture and even executions. So, he is now wanted by the United Nations for 'Crimes Against Humanity' and this warrant has been issued in the High Court for his arrest. He must have got wind that we were on his tail and he has just moved on. They will probably change their names again and disappear into the suburbs of Brisbane, Sydney or Melbourne. But we'll get him eventually."

After they'd gone I turned to Damian. "I hope they don't get him," I said. "I don't care what he did in Rhodesia. This is Australia and things are different here. Anyway the native Africans were not blame-free either. I read about it in the paper. They were raping and pillaging. Burning farmsteads and crops and killing the white settlers. No wonder the

Rhodesian military get a bit heavy handed with them. I think they should forget it all and move on. What do you think?"

I ask you, Dear Reader, the same question.

Where on Earth Have You Been?

by Rick Coy

Or as Ryan would have said "Where's youse bin?" to which I would reply, trying surreptitiously to correct his syntax and his accent by a subtle joke, "Which bin, the red, the yellow or the green?". Right over his head! He would look at me oddly as though to say "Sometimes I just don't get you!" Ryan is as thick as shit. Dog shit. But Ryan, as we were growing up, was the only friend I had.

We lived on an industrial estate. All around our house were factories, sheds, yards and all sorts of other mysterious buildings. I said to Dad, "Why don't we move?"

"Move? Why would we move? This is convenient." It was true. It was convenient. The main road was just at the end of the street with loads of buses which went straight into town. I went to a "decent" school on the other side of the city. My bus, the 174, stopped just around the corner. Mum sometimes used the 174 as well because it went into the city first. She worked at the bank. In the head office. I never knew what she really did. It was complicated, she said.

But I understood that she had broken through the glass ceiling. That was Dad's joke. He loved to tease Mum about her earning lots of money for doing "Stuff all!" His business was up the street from our house. He drove his BMW the few yards to work when he could quite easily have walked.

His firm made cement products. Well, Grandpa had established the business back in the fifties. He had rented a shed, put in his cement mixers, molds and frames; and he was away. When he was well established and starting to produce garden ornaments as well as pavers and blocks, he had bought the block of land on which our house stood. It was for his true love, Grandma.

She didn't mind living close to the business. She could keep her eye on Grandpa. She'd take his lunch up every day, stay in the office when he had to go out in the truck and, according to Dad, kept her eye on the books too. In our family Mum never "kept her eyes on the books" once Dad had inherited the business. She had nothing to do with Dad's business. The only time she would make any comment at all was if Dad got cement dust on his suits.

Ryan lived on the estate too. His mother cleaned the offices of various businesses, including ours. I never knew his dad. He'd "taken off" when Ryan and I were both little. We played together because there was no-one else. Ryan's house was a ramshackle hut up the street, just past Dad's cement products factory.

I hardly ever went to Ryan's house. He always came to mine. We had a pool, loads of playground equipment and as we got older, a billiards room in the basement. When you are little, it's not just that you are extra forgiving about other kids, but really you are unaware of any differences.

For example, little kids are colour blind when it comes to making friends at kindy or pre-school. That acceptance continues for quite a long time. That's why you see gangs of multi-coloured teenagers hanging around at the mall. It's only later that prejudices, partialities and xenophobia sets in. It was the same with Ryan and me.

I knew he wasn't as bright as me. I would have to read things to him and calculate the change when we went to the shop. But he was fun to play with. He would do anything I asked him to, and we would get into all kinds of mischief together. Mum tolerated him. She knew it was me leading him on; not Ryan being a bad influence. She thought the friendship would die once I went to a private school on the other side of the city. Ryan attended the state high school just up the main road. But our friendship continued. It's proximity as much as anything else, I suppose.

There was a factory next door to our house. I didn't know what they manufactured. At some sites around the estate, it was obvious what was being manufactured. It might even have a sign outside that advertised what they made. Not so at our neighbours. There wasn't even a business name outside. No sign at all. Just a letter box that said "No.18 Crankshaft St." Sometimes box vans would reverse into their yard and through the roller door into the factory. Then, the door would roll up and as the van left it would roll down before you could see what went on inside.

I asked Dad what they made. He said, "Oh! Just stuff. Don't bother yourself. And stay away from the yard and the factory. And don't talk to anyone who works there." What!!? That made me even more curious. I determined to find out what was manufactured within those factory walls.

One day, Ryan and I were kicking a soccer ball about on the back lawn. Never a very accurate kick, Ryan booted the ball over the chain mail fence that surrounded next door's factory. We had a six foot colour bond fence around our house and above that the said chain mail fence soared a further eight feet. It usually saved any balls from our side from going over into their yard but this time, due to Ryan's incompetence, there went our ball!

We climbed up onto an ornamental cement bench (one of Dad's catalogue specials) and watched our precious soccer ball bounce across their yard and with one final bounce, drop into a skip over by their back door. Ryan and I looked at each other and then back over at the skip. Tennis balls or other small rubber balls, if they went over, we wouldn't worry too much. There's always another one ... but our precious soccer ball ... that was too much.

As we stared in silence over the fence, wondering what to do, the back door opened and a rough looking man, carrying a bin came out. He tipped the bin into the skip and went back inside the door. I heard Ryan breathe "Shit!!" I looked at him because the sight of a man emptying a bin didn't warrant such a serious reaction.

"What's up?" I asked.

"I know him" replied Ryan. "That's Carver Cavinski. He's a mate of one of Mum's boyfriends."

"So?" I asked.

"He's called 'Carver' because he modifies people's faces if they don't pay their debts. He's just come out of the slammer."

"Oh!" I said. That made a difference but I wasn't sure what that difference was. I still wanted to retrieve my precious soccer ball. Also, in the back of my mind was the question, "What do they make over there?" I'm not sure whether it was the ball or my curiosity that triggered my next move. "We have to go over there and get it, Carver or not." I said.

"Are you kidding!?" exclaimed Ryan. "We can't go over there, you never know what they make, it could be drugs or anything and we don't know what they will do if they catch us. I don't want my face rearranged by Carver Cavinski!" There was silence for a moment.

Then, "Come on," I ordered. "I want my ball and you have to come because you kicked it over there."

The front gate of the factory next door was closed, but it wasn't locked. We opened it a little way and slipped through. There didn't seem to be anyone about. It took only a moment to scuttle around the side of the building and run, crouched down, along the wall to the skip by the back door. The skip was much bigger than it looked from our yard. The sides were about six foot high.

"Shit!" said Ryan again.

"Come on," I said. "I'll give you a leg up." I lifted Ryan up the side of the skip and onto the top edge. I asked him, "Can you see it?"

"Yes!" he replied. "It's over there. You'll have to come up too otherwise I won't be able to climb out." He reached down, grabbed my wrist and helped me up onto the edge of the bin beside him. I watched him jump down and pick up the ball.

Just as he picked it up I heard a noise. Quickly I dropped down beside him. We froze against the side of the skip. A load of plastic packaging showered down on top of us. Then some more. Cardboard too. And polystyrene buds and packaging tape. We stayed quite still. When we heard the door bang shut and silence return, we made a quick move. I legged him up onto the top again and I looked around for the ball. It was still there, where he dropped it but covered by all that packaging. I grabbed it and handed it up to him.

With difficulty, and clutching the ball to his chest with one hand, he helped me back up on to the top of the skip. We jumped down and scuttled back the way we had come. No time to sneak a look inside the factory. As we turned into our driveway, Dad arrived in his car. That was unusual. I smelled a rat.

Dad slid out of his car. "What have you two been up to?" he asked. I could tell that he already knew so I decided that truthfulness was the best policy.

"We went over there to get our soccer ball." I said.

"I know," he said. "Maurice rang me to say that he had intruders in his yard."

"You know him?" I asked.

"Of course," said Dad. "They manufacture kitchens, wardrobes and all sorts of cupboards."

"Why the secrecy then?" I asked.

"Because they make them from pre-cut parts and flat-pack materials imported from Malaysia. People think they make them from local materials and to specification." Dad replied.

"But we saw Carver Clavinski over there." Chipped in Ryan.

"Yes!" said Dad, "Maurice likes to help ex-cons and give them a fresh start. That's why I don't want you going over there. I'm not as convinced as Maurice of their good intentions. Now! One, don't go over there again. And two, don't tell your mother."

But, right on cue, the lady herself arrived. She took one look at our dishevelled state and asked, “Where on earth have you been?” Dad told her immediately and once he had brought his cleaner up to date, both Ryan and I were grounded.

Grounded! That’s the story of my life, I suppose.

I Wish I'd Never Met Ryan Daly

by Rick Coy

There are various ways two people can meet. Some good, some not so good. For example, two people meeting at an airport. One may be leaving and the other is sad. Or one might be coming home after a time away and both are ecstatic at seeing one another again. My meeting with Ryan Daly was not like that at all. Nor was it "We'll meet for coffee", or lunch or any meeting like that. It was neither pleasurable nor hostile. It just happened.

I found myself in a sort of waiting room. White walls! White furniture! My companion was a stranger. We glanced at each other surreptitiously and then at the clerk standing in front of the desk in his white suit.

"Welcome," he said, then looking at me, "Name?"

I felt compelled to answer properly. I was half tempted to answer, "Yes! I have a name, but it's mine, so use your own." But I didn't. The compulsion to answer properly was too strong. "Watkins. Harry Watkins."

"Mmm!" murmured the clerk staring into his huge ledger. There was a pause and then, turning to my companion, "And yours?"

My companion obviously felt the same compulsion. "Ryan Daly." Prompt and direct.

The clerk ran his finger down some list in his ledger. "You don't seem to be listed here," he said. "Are you sure you are a couple of Eve's?"

I heard Ryan's sharp intake of breath and assumed he didn't like being called 'An Eve'. I stepped in quickly to avoid an incident developing. "I don't know what you mean by 'An Eve', and I can really only speak for myself, but I don't think either of us fall into that category."

The clerk looked a little non-plussed. "You could be a couple of 'Buggers' I suppose. That would explain why you're not on my list."

This time Ryan did step forward. "I'll 'bugger' you," he said, raising his fist. I took hold of his elbow to restrain him.

The clerk glanced up. "It's alright," he said. "Sometimes this whole process is a bit confusing at first. He can't strike me. It's not allowed."

Now it was Ryan's turn to look non-plussed.

"Let me explain," said the clerk. "You have arrived at the Yoo-Ve. That's U.V.E. 'Unexpected Violent Exit'. But you aren't on my list so you must belong to some other category. I thought possibly B.U.G.A., that's 'Big Unexpected Gruesome Accident'. Or you might be an E.V.E., that's 'Expected Violent Exit'. You could be in there instead. I'll soon find out." He touched a button on the desk and spoke into a microphone. "I have a couple of newcomers and they're not on my list."

A speaker crackled. "Names?"

"Harry Watkins and Ryan Daly."

"Ah!" said the speaker, "They are supposed to be in Ripper. Sorry about that! Can you send them over there and I'll get someone to meet them."

"What the fuck is 'Ripper'?" demanded Ryan.

"Reproachable Inevitable Punishable Accident."

I could see Ryan was becoming belligerent again. So I asked quickly, "How many categories have you got?"

"Oh! Thousands. It's the way we sort everyone out. By the way you come here, you see. Your exit was by accident, but it was inevitable and reproachable."

"But why are we being punished?" I asked. "Is this Hell? I don't think I deserve that. I've had a good life and done loads of good in the world. I'm even a member of Amnesty International, and Greenpeace too."

"Ah! Yes! But you are here because of your driving."

"My driving?"

"Yes! You are a good driver, but you always drive too fast."

Ryan butted in. "He might be a wild driver, but I'm a professional. I drive for a living. Why am I here?"

"I'm afraid, Ryan, that your sin is one of driving too long without a break and therefore driving when you are tired."

"And that's why we are in Hell."

"Oh! No! There is no Hell, (or Heaven for that matter). Hell is only the knowledge that you could have done better in your lifetime. You now have to live with that knowledge."

"Oh! I can live with that knowledge. I've had to. I have had to get to my destinations quickly. To deliver my goods. So I won't be late. Or so I don't keep people waiting. It's quite justifiable really."

"I'm sorry," said the clerk, "But there is no justification possible. No rationalisation here either. Only the truth is possible. You'll just have to live with it."

I spoke up now. "But, if we are dead, what happened? Why are we here?"

"Oh! Sorry! Yes, I should have told you. Harry, you were going too fast, and you, Ryan, you were half asleep at the wheel of your truck. You met on a bend, head on."

"Shit!" I thought. "I wish I'd never met Ryan Daly."

I Was Wondering...
by Rick Coy

Charlie was a plumber. That's irrelevant really and Charlie is superfluous to this story, but he was there at the time so, in the interests of accuracy, I need to start with him.

When I was serving my time, not in gaol you idiot, my apprenticeship, I worked for Metro Plumbing Services and Charlie was one of their tradesmen. If I was assigned to him, it was our custom, if we were in the North Eastern suburbs, to stop the van outside the St Peters Bakery, which is on the North East Road near Tea Tree Gully and have a bit more breakfast before we arrived at the job. This particular morning we had a job at the eastern end of Hancock Road so Charlie rubbed his hands with glee and the next thing I knew we were inside the Bakery, by the roaring open fire, and Charlie had ordered muffins and coffee for us both. I stood with my back to the fire, "Warming the hole of my body," as Charlie put it, when three women came in.

Actually, it was only later, when Charlie related the sad, sad story to the others that it came out that there were three of them. I only saw HER!

She was probably a little older than me, in her early twenties, but she was really something. Statuesque, that's implies she was tall, beautiful and had an aura of great dignity. She was a 'classic'. That means she was well dressed, of classical beauty and she carried herself as though she owned everything around her.

She chose a table for them all, sat in a chair, and swivelled round to look at the menu chalked on the wall. As she swivelled, her long hair swung and the action accentuated her figure. I was smitten immediately. My mouth fell open and a glazed look came into my eyes. That's what Charlie told the others that same day when we got back to the yard.

In profile her face was perfect; smooth forehead, perfect nose and a chin neither determined nor weak. Perfect.

She had "Come to bed eyes" Charlie told the others, "Pillows under each!"

"She did not!" I leapt to her defence. "She had high cheek bones and huge almond eyes. No bags; just perfect skin." The others laughed. I knew Charlie was winding me up but I carried on regardless. I guessed, correctly, that Charlie would make a big deal of me going across and asking her out. He put me up to it from the start.

"If you're so smitten," he had said, "You have to grab the 'Bull by the Horns'. Get over there and ask he out. Nothing ventured, nothing gained."

I knew he'd label me a 'chicken' if I didn't and I wanted neither the present ribbing nor the upcoming humiliation before the others. I knew Charlie of old.

So I sauntered over to their table. I was really dressed to impress, in my 'Hi-Vis' duffle coat and my 'Crows' cap and I was conscious of my 'steel-capped' work boots, but, as I said before, we were on our way to a job, sometimes you just can't have the perfect situation, you have to make the best of what you've got.

"Excuse me, Miss," I began. "I was wondering, may I pay for your coffee, or even shout you some breakfast?"

"No thanks! We're fine."

She didn't even look at me ... I was dismissed.

"You can order me a cappuccino." said one of the others; giggling and looking at her friend. I ignored her and continued to look at THE ONE.

"I would appreciate a positive response," I said. "After all, I'd like to take you out to dinner, and, of course, if things work out, you may become the mother of my children!" It was an old, old pick-up line but it stopped her in her tracks. She looked at me properly for the first time.

"I don't think so!" she said, "on either count. Now, will you please leave us alone and get off to whatever mundane task you do in order to earn the meagre living that will keep you in the poverty and deprivation into which you so obviously belong." How can someone, sitting down, look down her nose at someone standing up? I don't know, but she managed it.

"May I leave my card?" I asked. "In case you change your mind."

I fished in my top pocket and pulled out one of Metro Plumbing's cards which we always carry, under instructions from management, and a pen. I wrote my name and phone number in the space provided and held it out to her. She didn't even look at it, but one of the others took my card and just stared at me until I turned away and went back to Charlie.

"It was a humiliating experience!" Charlie grinned at the others. "Even I was embarrassed!"

On the following Monday morning, Jason from the front office, came up to us in the yard. "The Boss wants to see you two in his office, immediately."

"Oh! Shit!" said Charlie, "What have we done now?"

The Boss looked up from his desk. "Charlie, when you leave for a job, you are on the firm's time. 'Travel time' is unproductive work time, as you well know, and must be kept to a minimum. So it does not include time off for breakfast at the St Peters Bakery. This is your second formal warning, Charlie, one more and I will dock your wages."

"Second warning!" exclaimed Charlie.

"Yes!" said the Boss. "Don't forget that incident two years ago with the attractive widow in Modbury North. That was number one, so you now only have one life left!"

Charlie didn't say anything more, which is unusual for Charlie, but the Boss waved him away. I turned to follow him. "Not you!" said the Boss. I turned back, my stomach sinking. He reached for a folder on his desk. One of the firm's cards was attached to the top corner with a paper clip. He slipped it from under the clip and handed it to me. I immediately recognised the name and mobile number written in the space provided. The memory of my humiliation came flooding back. I was about to say something like, "Sorry about that, but ..." when the Boss grinned at me. "That woman you tried to race off was Mitchell Fairburn's daughter."

I knew of Mitchell Fairburn. He is a big developer. Nothing less than multi-million dollar projects.

"He was at the dinner table with his wife and daughter and was telling them that Advanced Plumbing had let him down and he needed a new plumbing firm for his latest project, and his daughter said, 'I know a good plumbing firm' and fished your card out of her purse. He came in here on Friday and we discussed the project. Ten town houses. Two stories. En-suite and toilet upstairs, bathroom, toilet, laundry and kitchen downstairs. We discussed it then, and he just rang ... we got the job. At least six months work. You and Charlie can do it. Don't let me down."

www.ingramcontent.com/pod-product-compliance
Lightning Source LLC
Chambersburg PA
CBHW070313120726
47910CB00007B/2468

* 9 7 8 0 9 9 4 5 9 9 0 4 9 *